So I think I'll become a musician

An autobiography in nine movements by

Louis Mordish

Stainer & Bell

British Library Cataloguing-in-Publication Data.
A catalogue record for this book is available from the British Library

ISBN 0 85249 808 X

Printed in Great Britain by Galliard (Printers) Ltd, Great Yarmouth.

Contents

Opening bars

If my parents had been richer, I would probably have been American. They were Russian Jews, and like so many of their contemporaries, left the anti-semitic persecutions of Czarist Russia in the early part of this century to find freedom in another country. Those who could saved enough money for a passage to America, with its promise of opportunity and its hunger for immigrants to develop its enormous territories. Others preferred to settle nearer the homeland. Mother and Father came over in a cattle boat from one of the Baltic ports, landed in London and found themselves in the Jewish ghetto of Whitechapel. They could not afford the fares to America, so they decided to make their home here in England.

Naturally, my very first recollections are of this world in which I was born – a world of hard-working people, poverty-stricken and strongly religious, whose knowledge of the world beyond their own little ghetto was virtually non-existent. I was about two-and-a-half years old, climbing up a flight of wooden stairs to reach a little room at the top of the house. An elderly man with a long beard and wearing a cap was sorting pieces of cloth on a wire mesh table. (He was probably my grandmother's second husband; they had both come to England soon after my parents arrived, but returned to Russia after a couple of years.) I remember him saying to me, 'Go and play with the little wooden cotton-reels' – in Yiddish of course.

I recall walking between my parents with my arms stretched upwards and holding their hands, jumping up and down and swinging while crossing the road over tramlines, with mother holding the side of her long skirt off the wet road. I remember looking into a shop window full of Singer sewing machines, and eating salt-beef sandwiches with pickled cucumbers in Bloom's shop at the corner of Brick Lane and Old Montague Street. I also recall being with my father in a barber shop when he had a row with the barber, who was

1

using father's own shaving-mug for another customer. In those days there were very few safety razors. Working-men went to the barber's once or twice a week to have their beards shaved with the old-fashioned cut-throat razor. Most customers had their own shaving mugs which would be kept in the shop, lining the shelves. Men usually paid regular visits on definite days each week and on this occasion my father had gone to the barber on a different day from his usual custom!

There were no musicians in my family as far as I'm aware. It was a typical Jewish immigrant background of poverty and hard work. My father's original name was Berish-Wolf, anglicized by a friend to 'Barnett'. (Many years later I discovered from a copy of his birth certificate forwarded from a Polish relative that his name was given as Beresz-Wolf Mudrysz.) He was born around 1878 in Dubno, at that period a town in Russian-Poland. My grandfather, a carpenter, died at a very early age leaving a young widow and four small children. My father was about four at the time. My grandmother found it very difficult to cope with a large family, even though her relatives all helped. So at the age of nine, he went to live with Uncle Isaac, in whose workshop he began to learn the art of tailoring. Then, some years later, the whole family – uncle, mother, sisters and brother – moved from Dubno to the Jewish quarter of Odessa, in the Ukraine.

Father carried on working until the time when, as a young man, he was conscripted into the Russian Army, doing his national service for five years. Ironically, although Jewish people were treated as second-class citizens with few legal rights, the Russian authorities still claimed their first-born sons for military service. This would have been about the time of the Russo-Japanese war. I recall him telling me – years later – how astonished he was to learn that our English royalty moved freely among the people. In Russia, whenever the Imperial family travelled, soldiers lined the route, keeping crowds at a distance. He himself had often been on such duties.

As second-class citizens, Jews were confined to ghettos in the large towns, and needed special permission to live outside. However, most Jewish people lived in villages, in a poverty-stricken existence as small-time tradesmen and artisans. These villages were sentimentally referred to as 'shtetls' – small towns. Travelling

2

between the larger towns was very limited, and confined mainly to pedlars and similar people.

With no formal schooling of any kind, the only education for men was in Hebrew, reading and translating the Pentateuch (the Five Books of Moses), and studying the Talmud and Torah, and the Jewish way of life with its customs and traditions. Girls received no education whatsoever either from the civil authorities or the rabbis. Usually they could not even read or write Hebrew, for the whole of their upbringing was centred around the art of home-making for an early and successful arranged marriage. The teachers were the village rabbi and his assistants, and their school the 'cheder', and later the 'yeshiva' – parts of the synagogue set aside for learning and study. The everyday language was Yiddish and the knowledge of the Russian language fairly basic. There was little need of it in these closed communities, where the rabbi was not only the teacher of young people, but also the authority, guide, judge, and complete spiritual leader and counsellor for the whole community.

My mother was named Nachoma Kantrowitz and was born in a 'shtetl' called Pokatilev, near Kiev. She had three sisters and two brothers, and her father was a tailor. Like everyone else they suffered from the frequent pogroms and persecutions. She told me of one occasion when the family hid in the cellar for three days while drunken peasants went on the rampage. Afterwards, when all was quiet, they emerged to find piles of Jewish corpses. Characteristically, the authorities did nothing, apart from sending in sword-waving Cossacks after the pogroms to frighten the Jewish people still further.

When she was nineteen, her father, now in his early fifties, became ill and was treated in an Odessa hospital. (How it was that a poor Jewish tailor got into a big town hospital we shall never know.) Not wishing to be on his own so far from his family, he took his favourite daughter – my mother – with him. Supporting herself as a dress-maker, she lodged with a family and was able to pay frequent visits to the hospital. When grandfather died in the hospital, my mother did not return to Pokatilev. She had already met my father, who was distantly related to the family with whom she was staying, and had fallen in love. He was just about to go into the army. Mother waited five years for him while he was on service. During this time, her mother and younger brother died, her elder brother Joseph

3

emigrated to America, and her sisters married – so there was no point in going home anyway.

This was a period of savage pogroms in that part of Russia. When my father left the army, he and his bride-to-be decided to leave the country to find freedom. They married under Jewish religious auspices, and their marriage certificate still survives, printed in Russian and Hebrew. But only the Hebrew part was completed and signed. The other was left blank, as they feared that if the authorities found out, they would stop them from leaving the country. The family with whom she had been living were also emigrating, so they travelled together by train from Odessa to one of the Baltic ports. There they boarded the cattle-boat, on which the owners had built shoddy compartments to accommodate passengers and livestock.

The overcrowded vessel took three days to make its journey across the North Sea to the Port of London. The passengers gathered their few belongings together – bundles of bedding and pillows, clothes and precious personal belongings such as the important candlesticks for lighting the Sabbath and holy-day candles. Then they descended the gangway and stepped on to British soil. At that time England and the USA had an 'open door' policy; no passports were necessary, but all immigrants had to be officially interviewed. When it came to my father's turn he was asked his name. Any documents he might have carried would have been in Russian; so it was a matter of sheer chance that the particular official decided to spell it in the way it is written today – Mordish.

Father's cousin, the daughter of Uncle Isaac who'd brought him up, had married some years earlier and emigrated to London. She lived in Hanbury Street. He had her address, and after seeing that my mother and the accompanying family were safely resting in the Jewish Immigration Shelter in Leman Street (an institution where immigrants stayed temporarily until they found accommodation, usually with other immigrant families), he went with another young man to find her. There was no language problem; it seemed that everybody in the East End of London was an immigrant, and they all spoke Yiddish. There was great surprise when they finally met. She had no knowledge that he was coming, but temporary accommodation was soon found in her house. My parents moved into one room, and father found a tailoring job in a workshop. He told me how hard he worked, both to impress his new employers and to earn

4

a living wage. He put in many hours every day, and at the end of his first week was rewarded with the princely sum of one golden half-sovereign, 10s. in the money of the time.

Eventually my parents found a two-roomed dwelling in Brady Street Buildings, their first home. Brother Jack was born there, and I followed soon after.

Though people were very poor in the area where I was born, there was an atmosphere of life and excitement. Everyone was working class: tailors, cutters, machinists, pressers, buttonhole makers, trouser makers, cabinet makers, cobblers and cigarette makers. All had the same problem: trying to make a living! As in every community, some people were more successful than others in their working life. Imaginative and adventurous men opened up businesses, mostly in the garment trade, creating more and more sweat-shops where others like my father would toil in hot, stuffy conditions. Although the workers grumbled and cursed about them, these were still preferable to the atmosphere of persecution in Russia and Poland.

And the Sabbath was the Sabbath! There were many synagogues where the members of the small communities regularly went to pray, and where they continued to carry on their studies. The religious atmosphere was always very strong, and the Jewish Sabbath, Saturday, was definitely a holy day: no one worked; shops were closed; people dressed in their best clothes and walked to their destinations. No one would dream of travelling on a bus or tram. Women did not cook but kept food from the previous day warm in an oven. Most men went to the synagogue on Saturday mornings, and when the Sabbath was over, families would visit each other. There were strong friendships, especially among the *landsleit* – people who came from the same or nearby towns – and as there was no TV, radio, hi-fi or video, people visited each other far more than today for the obvious social reasons of company and conversation.

There were Yiddish newspapers including *Die Zeit* (The Times), which continued for many years. Placards, posters, names and signs on shop fronts were all in Yiddish. There was a Yiddish Theatre called *The Pavilion* in the Whitechapel Road, and another called the *Grand Palais* in the Commercial Road. I recall being taken as a very young child to *The Pavilion* by my parents. It was a longish hall – or it seemed to me at the time. Before the play commenced, and during

5

the intervals, people in the balcony would have long shouting conversations with their friends below, shouting louder than their neighbours to make themselves heard. The ladies, all wearing big picture hats, would often stick them to the wall using their large hat-pins as hooks. Professor Staub was the orchestra leader, and I can even remember one of the songs in a musical play, sung by the leading man, which was a strange mixture of Yiddish and bad English:

Oy   I   love she.___   Oy, Oy, Oy, I   love she.___   Wie sie geht, und wie sie steht.

On Saturday evenings after the Sabbath, if the weather was fine, people would promenade along Whitechapel High Road, meeting their friends for conversation. A simple and inexpensive way of spending an evening.

When I was about four, our family moved to No 4 Booth Street. I carried a long broom and walked behind the hand-cart which carried our meagre furniture. At this new address both my brother and I caught measles. When we had recovered, my father bought us each a toy rifle with rubber suction sticks. Clad in our long combinations we fired them at targets hanging on the door while jumping up and down in bed.

About a year or so later we moved to No 17 Fournier Street where we had two first-floor rooms. It was there I first saw a piano. At that time my mother was pregnant. Having two boys already, Father used to say that the next child would be a girl – and she would learn to play the piano. So he went out and bought one on hire purchase at a shilling a week from a firm called Parker's in Bishopsgate. It was an old-fashioned type, with candlesticks and inlaid designs on the front. By what standards my father judged the instrument I shall never know – he couldn't play. Probably he just liked the look of it, and a shilling a week was all he could afford. In later years I discovered that it had a heavy, unreliable action and a cheap, jangling tone. But who was to know at the time whether it was good or bad? For me, it was the only piano I ever practised on, and we kept it until I was in my early twenties. It was years before I learnt to recognize a decent instrument.

One day, our family went to visit some friends who had a little salt-beef shop in Leman Street. While I was playing and sliding about

6

on the polished tile floor, I slipped and broke my ankle. I was taken off to the London Hospital (on foot, naturally, as no-one could afford a cab). I still remember father carrying me while I had my arms around his neck, and I also recall the blue flashing light of the X-ray machine. My leg was put into a plaster-of-paris mould which I wore for ten weeks.

One of our two rooms was the kitchen and the other a combined parlour and bedroom which also contained the piano. As mother had her housework to attend to, she would often place two chairs and a pillow in front of the piano, seat me on the pillow with my leg stretched out, and leave me to strum and amuse myself on the instrument. Somehow, I learnt to play the melody of the *Donau Wellen* waltz – probably with one finger – now known as 'The Anniversary Waltz' and used in the film *The Jolson Story*. I can certainly remember my parents trying to dance in our little bedroom, with my father singing while I strummed the tune. Another old waltz which he used to sing (I always thought he had a very good voice) and which I learnt from him, was *Dream of Autumn* by Archibald Joyce. To this day, whenever I hear those melodies, I get quite sad and emotional and picture my dear parents dancing in that bedroom-cum-parlour-cum-music room.

One morning I was told that I had a little sister. Going to the bedside, I was shown the baby to kiss. In those days most confinements were at home. I know she was named Clara, but tragically she died when about ten days old.

From Fournier Street we moved again, this time to No 5 Spelman Street, where we had four rooms: a tiny kitchen and scullery in the cellar, and two rooms on the ground floor. The front cellar-room was lit by light from the pavement-grating above the window. Being a ladies' tailor, father converted the front room into a workshop, with a large tailor's table, a machine and stool, a tailor's dummy and an ironing board. There was hardly room to walk around. The rear room was our bedroom and parlour complete with piano.

When I was about seven my father decided that I should learn the piano and I started taking lessons from a Miss Phillips, the daughter of a friend. I waded through *Smallwoods Piano Tutor*, made good progress, and learnt for about nine months. Then I fell ill during Pesach, the Passover Festival. My mother took me to see Dr Gaster, a highly respected East-End practitioner, who immediately diagnosed diphtheria. I was sent to St Anne's Hospital in Tottenham where I stayed for sixteen weeks and my life was saved by an emergency operation, a tracheostomy. For about nine or ten weeks I was on the danger list, and needed the rest of the stay for recovery and convalescence. My parents came to see me twice every day, and I can still visualize them coming into the ward wearing their white hospital-overalls.

And here is a fantastic story – and true! On the night I had the operation, my mother couldn't sleep. Eventually, she got up very early in the morning to go to the hospital. She knew something was the matter with her 'Labele' (my name in Yiddish). She took the first tram of the day and sat next to a very old Jewish woman who started up a conversation.

'Where are you going so early?' she asked.

Mother replied, 'I'm going to the hospital where my little boy is ill.'

'Oh,' said the woman, 'I'm also going there. I'm a *Vacher* and I've been informed that a little Jewish boy has died in the hospital.'

A *Vacher* in the Jewish faith is a 'watcher': a person who sits by a dead person, watching over the body until it is removed for burial. I believe this custom has disappeared among modern Jewry. Imagine how my mother felt until she reached the hospital!

When I had recovered and was due to go home, my parents came for me in style. They hired a horse-drawn cab with curtains over the little windows, and we made the journey back to Spelman Street in a manner befitting such an important occasion. I wasn't altogether happy when I left the hospital buildings. Two nurses helped me walk to where my parents and brother were waiting by the cab – and they were all crying. Not understanding that their tears were of relief and joy, I thought they were crying because they didn't want me home. Back at the house, the neighbours came to welcome us – especially me! I remember mother happily carrying me around while various women 'bought' me for a halfpenny! This is an old Jewish superstition. A young person who has recovered from an illness can be 'bought' from the family in which the illness was contracted, thereby assuring future good health. Once again I cried, because I didn't want to be sold to anyone.

Following my return from hospital, my parents stopped my piano lessons. I never discovered why. Perhaps they couldn't afford the current rate of 7s. 6d. per term. However, I kept on playing, and I began to develop a fair beginner's technique. Moreover, as I had learnt to read music before my illness, I could wade through popular songs and similar pieces. Teenagers would buy copies of songs and bring them to me to play. My brother had begun to take violin lessons and between us (he was ten and I eight) we managed to make a sort of music. Jewish people, for some inexplicable reason, have always been drawn to the violin as a means of satisfying musical needs. Perhaps my parents, unable to afford lessons for both Jack and myself, had decided the violin would be the musical instrument in our family.

And there were other forms of entertainment. We all enjoyed street games, playing at cops and robbers, leapfrog and hopscotch, and with diabolos, marbles and spinning tops. A favourite game, called 'nuts', was played by boys competing against each other with cobnuts. Each boy knelt on the pavement kerb, a nut was placed against the wall of a house and all took turns in trying to hit it with another nut. The winner hit the target nut and kept all the others.

Our traditional East-end poverty also made us worthy of special help in the eyes of the authorities. At school in Chicksand Street we were occasionally provided with what were called 'happy evenings'. Tickets were given out to selected pupils or possibly even an entire class, and we would dutifully gather for our prescribed enjoyment. I remember going to the school hall, very bare and lit by gaslight, and sitting on a long wooden form with the other children to watch a Punch and Judy show, and conjuring from a man in a funny hat. We were each given a bag of sweets and an apple. Rather different from today's recreations.

Chiefly, however, there was the cinema, or 'the pictures' as we called them – a new form of entertainment. My local cinema was in Osborne Street, where I got in for a halfpenny. We all sat on long, hard forms in a very large room, staring up at the flickering black-and-white moving objects projected on to a dirty screen about three feet away. And I recall watching with fascination workmen laying a mosaic in the entrance of a brand new cinema, the Brick Lane Picture Palace, a building which was actually being built for 'the pictures' – no less than the eighth wonder of the world.

Cars were still very much a novelty in the East End. Our milkman, wearing a straw hat and striped apron, drove around in a pony and trap carrying a large churn of milk. Stopping at each house he took a smaller churn and measured out a pint or half-pint of milk with a long-handled ladle. When we were short of milk, mother would give me a jug and send me to a dairy in nearby Hope Street, where there were cows in the backyard. And sometimes I was allowed to ride with the milkman for a hundred yards. A real thrill. And how I was envied!

It was while we were living in Spelman Street that the Great War started. Several young men in the district were called up to the army. One lived in our house, where he and his mother occupied the other two rooms. I remember his coming home on leave, and watching, fascinated, as he wound his khaki puttees round his legs.

There were frequent air-raids – or we used to think they were frequent. We had 'blackouts', and were alerted by police and wardens blowing whistles and shouting to everyone to take cover. Later on, warning maroons were fired. We would run from our tiny houses to take shelter in the big houses on the other side of the street. There we would wait until the 'all clear' was given. Once, I saw a Zeppelin flying over London. I was playing in the street and saw an enormous cigar-shaped object in the sky. I can also recall the Silvertown explosion, when a munitions factory in Silvertown in the docklands area of the East End blew up, with terrible casualties.

The air raids continued into the last months of the war. By this time, we'd moved from the East End to Shepherds Bush, which seemed almost like being out in the country. However, the bombing went on to the end. Gently but urgently, my parents would wake us and, half asleep, we'd stumble to Osram's factory at Brook Green – regarded as a safe shelter. There, I would fall asleep in mother's arms, to be startled out of this rest by the sound of anti-aircraft guns.

In Shepherd's Bush we were now living in an area where English was the daily language. My parents were unable to speak it even passably well; like everybody else in our part of the East End, their language was Yiddish – the language I also learnt as a child. Until I started school at the age of three-and-a-half, I hardly ever heard anything else. Where I was brought up was really the transfer of a Russian-Jewish ghetto to London. Customs, manners, habits and religious observances were identical to those in the homeland.

Though we had moved, my parents remained strict observers of the Jewish way of life. I still recall with nostalgia the sanctity of Friday evenings, when Mother would spread a clean, white tablecloth covering a challah, or plaited loaf, on the table, light the Sabbath candles and after waving her hands gently over them, cover her eyes while she recited a benediction. Father would finish work at dusk on Fridays, and never at any time in his life did he ever work on a Saturday or on a high festival day. He would 'davan' or pray every morning before going to work, and was joined by Jack and me when we were Bar Mitzvahed. Every morning we put on our tallesim or prayer-shawls and tefillin or phylacteries, and the three of us would pray together in the kitchen. This ritual continued until I was about nineteen, and seemed the normal thing to do.

When my brother Jack was Bar Mitzvahed, my parents decided to have a little reception for friends and distant relatives. (We had no near relatives at all, and to this day I have never known what it is to see an uncle or aunt or cousin.) There were about thirty people present, and it was held in the front room of the flat below. In the corner of the room was a little harmonium used by the owner of the flat, who was the choir-master at the local synagogue. While the guests were taking their places at the tables, the caterer, who was also Master of Ceremonies as well as the waiter, took me into a corner. 'They tell me you can play the piano,' he said, 'so you sit there by the organ and wait. When I announce your parents, they will come into the room arm in arm, followed by the Bar Mitzvah boy. And when I nod to you, I want you to play tum – tum-te-tum; tum – tum-te-tum.' I'd heard that tune vaguely before, and at the cue from the waiter, I dutifully played while the delighted guests applauded and banged on the tables. Later I was asked why I had played the 'Wedding March'.

Our new home had three rooms, one of which was very small, and a kitchen. But we still had to share the communal toilet and bathroom at the top of the house, often causing problems. There was no light in the toilet, and we had to take a lighted candle with us at night. Flats didn't exist for the ordinary working-class people. Families rented rooms in a house.

Soon after the Armistice, my father decided yet again to run one of our rooms into a workshop and work at home. As a journeyman tailor working for a number of shops, he would collect parcels of work from each one in order to work on them at home. In those days every district had its own small highstreet tailor-shop and anyone needing new clothes would have them made there. Using paper patterns as a guide, the shopkeepers cut the material and had the garment made up by outside workers, such as my father. Many times I collected or

11

delivered bundles, occasionally helping by removing basting-stitches with a bodkin. During the busy season he sat cross-legged on his table, stitching away. When I woke in the morning he was already at work, and when I went to bed at night he was still sewing.

Mother prepared and cooked the meals – there were no convenience foods then, and freezing was unknown. She also washed and ironed the laundry – in a copper boiler in the kitchen, shopped and scrubbed the floors; if she had a spare moment she would help father in the workshop. Small wonder that they kept the Sabbath holy: a day free from work. But in the slack season it was a different story, with no unemployment benefit or free medical care. When a man was out of work, there was nothing he could do except hope for the next busy season.

Though we were poor, when I was about eleven we were invited to spend a weekend at Westcliff with the same friends of my parents who owned the salt-beef shop where I'd had my accident. They'd prospered, and moved away from the East End. Naturally they wanted their friends to see how they'd improved their way of life.

We travelled from Fenchurch Street station. It was my first journey on a steam-train. We were overawed by the house, with its three bedrooms and carpeted stairs. We had to take our shoes off before walking up the cream-coloured runners. Such opulence and style! It was also my first glimpse of the sea. We looked out from the promenade at an enormous stretch of mud which almost reached the opposite side of the river-mouth. Westcliff is on the Thames estuary and strictly speaking is not a seaside town at all. But how was I to know? As I gazed out I thought, 'Is this what people go on holiday for? Is this the seaside and is that the sea?'

Meanwhile, my education was progressing. I'd been attending school at Addison Gardens, an ordinary London County Council school, from the time we'd moved to Shepherds Bush. I remember being involved in a couple of fights with other boys when I was called a 'dirty Jew-boy' and 'a stinking Sheeny' (I realized even then that anti-semitism was not the exclusive prerogative of Czarist Russia). At the age of eleven, I was transferred to William Street Central School (later called the West Kensington Central School) about a mile from home. As there was no bus route available, I had to make my way on foot, whatever the weather. I had quite a busy time in those days: prayers in the morning even before I was Bar Mitzvahed, running to school, running home for lunch as my parents forbade me to eat non-Kosher food, making my way home again, attending chedar each evening, then finding time for homework and piano practice.

I was top boy in my class and year. Parents were invited to attend the school and see their sons receive prizes. (This was a boys-only school; mixed schools were unknown for my age group.) I persuaded my parents to come and see me receive mine. My father was difficult to persuade as this was the 'season' and he could not really spare the time. But he did come along with my mother, and they sat at the back listening to the speeches and watching the prize-giving.

I received a book called *Stories of Natural History*. I remember my feeling of embarrassment when I noticed that although father had put on a tie for the occasion, he was still unshaven and in his working clothes. When I joined them and heard them speaking to other parents, I became aware how badly they spoke English, with limited vocabulary and non-existent grammar. Like all their contemporaries, they pronounced the letter 'W' as 'V', hence their 'vells', 'vots' and 'veres'. To this day I am ashamed for having felt so embarrassed, not to understand then what it actually cost my father to give up a morning's work.

At that time, children were able to leave school at the age of fourteen, although boys at the Central School were expected to stay until sixteen. Although I had never given any serious thought to my future, a schoolboy story had given me vague ideas about becoming a lawyer or barrister. Playing the piano was something quite apart from any career. Then, some weeks before my fourteenth birthday, my parents called me into the front room. It was a Saturday and father was wearing his Shabbat suit, collar and tie. (Even now I can recall the incident so vividly.) He said, word for word in Yiddish, 'Labele my child, I want to talk to you. You are now nearly fourteen years old and can soon leave school. I can't afford to keep you at school any longer. What would you like to do for a living?'

After some discussion, I said 'Well, I can play the piano a bit, so I think I'll become a musician.'
'In that case' replied my father, 'I'll try my best to help you and will pay for your lessons until you find a job.'

When I told my form-master I'd be leaving school at fourteen, he told the headmaster, Mr Dawson, who asked my father to call. At the interview, where I was present, Mr Dawson protested that I was

13

too bright to be ending my studies, but father replied that he couldn't afford to keep me at school any longer. Eventually an arrangement was made for me to try for a scholarship at The Bluecoat School, but father refused to let me take the examination because it was held on a Saturday morning. Moreover, when he saw a photograph of the uniform, he thought the school was a training for the Christian priesthood. That finally put an end to my studies.

Flickering shadows

And so in 1922, at the age of fourteen, I said farewell to scholarship and applied myself to daily piano practice for some weeks, before trying to find a job. My brother, aged sixteen, had somehow got into a small cinema-orchestra as second violinist. He played without pay, gaining experience. This was a very common situation; young musicians playing in orchestras for several months, learning the ropes, then finding a paid job somewhere. Orchestral leaders encouraged this unpaid work, either because they were getting paid by the owners of the cinemas to have an orchestra of a certain size and did not pay one of the musicians, or because it flattered them to have an augmented orchestra.

But this kind of unpaid apprenticeship was impossible for a pianist. Cinema orchestras consisted of any number of players from three upwards, depending on the size of the cinema. But they were all built around the piano, because it made the harmony and provided a complete sound. No leader dare have an inexperienced musician on the keyboard.

Nevertheless, although I despaired at first, without knowing it I had already acquired, by coincidence, quite a few skills needed for the job.

For some months I had tuition from an Italian who was then aged eighty-three. Having learnt to read some years earlier, I made good progress and quickly absorbed his teaching. But he was too old. His hands trembled and he could not show me what to do. My parents, musically ignorant, were persuaded by a well-meaning friend, equally ignorant, to entrust our musical tuition to the second violinist of the local music hall, a man who could not play the piano at all. His method of teaching was to put a copy of the 'Star Folio' collection of overtures, including such favourite pot-boilers as *Poet and Peasant*, *Raymond* and *Light Cavalry*, on the music stand, and let me struggle

15

through them. Meanwhile he scratched away on his fiddle. Many years later I discovered that some of these piano arrangements are actually impossible to play. Realizing at last that this man was a fraud, we found two proper professional musicians instead. They were both very capable performers in café orchestras, and both Dutchmen. My teacher was Isadore Snoek, my brother's Nathan de Jong. So, at the age of thirteen, I had my first proper piano lessons, having already developed a fair if unorthodox technique. By chance, my parents had some acquaintances whose son, a young man of about twenty-two, was trying to organize a dance for young Jewish people at a social club. He knew no professional musicians – how many people in the tailoring business did? So he and his committee gave the job of supplying music for dancing to Jack and me. For this Saturday-evening hop we received the princely sum of 10s.

On another occasion, before we went to our new teachers, there was a Sunday-evening concert at a synagogue hall where nearly all the people who entertained, members of the community or their children, were singers. The only non-vocal music available, other than the piano accompaniments, was that supplied by Jack and me. On the advice of our scratching violin-playing teacher, we played *Colonel Bogey* as the concert overture, which was announced with all due pomp and ceremony, while my parents sat in the audience beaming with pride, acknowledging the deferential looks of the envious listeners.

Cinema orchestras provided the only alternative form of orchestral music to that provided by the music hall. Musical accompaniment was an important means to create atmosphere in the silent films, and many excellent musicians earned their living by playing in such orchestras.

I had always visited the cinema regularly to follow the serials: cliff-hangers, which left the viewer in agonizing suspense at the end of each weekly part. Serials, such as *Tarzan of the Apes*, *The Son of Tarzan*, *The Lost City*, *Mystery of 13* and *The Broken Coin*. Their regular devotees lustily cheered the hero and just as enthusiastically booed the villain. The plot didn't really matter; as soon as anyone leapt on to a horse and galloped away, the cheers of the audience, usually very young boys and girls, drowned the musical accompaniment. I heard the exciting music of Auber's overture *Masaniello* for fights, the heroic march from the same work as the

16

hero's theme and 'The Four Indian Love Lyrics' and 'The Egyptian Ballet' for Eastern scenes. Of course, I didn't know the titles then, but I recognized the pieces immediately I met them in later years.

This was long before the days of the Wurlitzer, but there was one cinema in the district which attracted countless numbers of people. The posters outside proudly proclaimed that it even had an organ with a human voice: actually an organ stop known as the Vox Humana with a tremulant effect which was considered a novelty. The rest of the organ was an ordinary church instrument.

In fact, many people would visit cinemas not only to see films, but also to sit with their eyes closed, listening to the music. Unlike today, when supermarkets, cafés, railway stations, and transistor radios inundate us with music wherever we go, and whether we like it or not.

A most exhilarating experience was to sit in a cinema during a comedy film and hear the enormous volume of laughter. I recall that during a showing of Harold Lloyd's *Safety Last* the orchestra was inaudible, although it was scraping away at light overtures like *Lutzspiel* and *French Comedy Overture*, both by a composer named Kela Bela. They might just as well have stopped playing, for the sheer volume of laughter drowned everything. I have never heard such sustained belly-laughs since. And the laughter was genuine, not 'canned'.

My parents were desperately anxious to help us with our musical education, even though they themselves knew so little about the subject. They'd never heard of a symphony orchestra, but discovered that there were concerts every Sunday at the Queen's Hall, near Oxford Circus, and that some people were allowed in free. This meant getting there very early and queuing at the stage door for the limited number of seats available, immediately behind the orchestra on the platform.

I was about thirteen, and trembling with anticipation on my first visit to a symphony concert. Mother thought I was ill and wanted to cancel our visit, but I persuaded her not to. And so, that Sunday evening, we all went to the Queen's Hall and queued with the other impoverished music-lovers. I found myself sitting behind the bass-trombone, although at the time I did not know the name of the instrument. Not exactly the best place to hear a symphony orchestra; indeed, one was virtually a member of the orchestra, and I could, in

17

fact, read his orchestral parts. We had no programmes, but I remembered the main themes and years later discovered that two of the works played were Elgar's 'Enigma Variations' and Bizet's *L'Arlésienne* Suite. The conductor was Sir Henry Wood. It was a memorable occasion, and as we travelled home on the top deck of a bus, my mind was a jumbled impression of music and musicians.

So with no idea of how to start in the musical profession, I walked from cinema to cinema, asking each Musical Director if a pianist was needed, and always receiving the same reply: 'You're too young, sonny, come back in a couple of years when you're older.'

It was heart-breaking. Every evening I would come home vowing to try again tomorrow in a different district, and then start the rounds once more. Then my luck changed. I visited a very small cinema – I think it was called the Star Cinema in Hammersmith Road – where the Musical Director was a very short, stout lady in charge of an orchestra of two: herself as pianist and a young violinist. She insisted on being addressed as 'Madame'. She was very kind, heard me play during the film, then told me she could find me a place in her orchestra playing the Mustel organ – a variety of large harmonium. I would be playing from cello parts, flute parts or any others she had available. There would be a three-month trial without pay, to see how I got on. But it was a start in the profession.

Months later my parents told me that when I went to work on my very first day, resplendent with straw-hat, pince-nez and silver-topped ebony walking stick (a Barmitzvah present) they watched me from a window with tears of joy and pride. Father said, 'Thank God my son won't be in the soul-destroying tailoring trade. He'll be a gentleman.'

For three months I played without pay, gaining experience as agreed. The cinema was open only in the evenings, and every Friday I did the whole of the film accompaniment on my own as a relief pianist while the other members of the orchestra had a day off. I was fourteen at the time, and most of the music had to be improvised while I watched the screen to fit the changing scenes. The accompaniments were probably dreadful; but few people would have been knowledgeable enough to notice.

After three months, Madame told me she was very pleased, and started to pay me for my work: a half-crown per week. I was very proud. This was the first money I had ever earned apart from playing

18

at the dance, for which Jack and I received the money between us. This lasted for some weeks, and then to my delight, Madame said she would now start paying me 10s. a week. This was very encouraging news, and this increase continued for a month or so. Then one day she suddenly informed me that she had been paying me out of her own pocket and could no longer afford to do so. I would have to leave in a week's time. I'd got the sack. However, she was very kind and told me she had spoken to a friend of hers who might be able to employ me, but I would have to give an audition.

So I went along to the Scala Cinema at Finsbury Park as arranged, where I duly gave my audition to the violinist-leader of the orchestra, Miss Pat O'Callaghan. The orchestra was actually accompanying the film at the time, so I sat at the Mustel organ and joined the five-piece orchestra in a number called 'Storm and Fire Music' by Zamecnik – a prolific composer for silent films. On the screen above my head I could see vivid tongues of flame destroying everything while I played:

I got the job, at a salary of 30s. a week for seven evenings. I was now fifteen, and studying with Mr Snoek, practising hard during the day and working in the evening.

After about six months, Miss O'Callaghan was offered another job. She took her orchestra with her, including my brother and me. And so it was that we went to play at the *La Bohème* cinema in the Mile End Road for the weekly salary of £2. 10s. each. Between us we brought £5 into the house. With my father's earnings it was a small fortune. We began to feel more secure and established.

In the early twenties, we were aware of a new phenomenon – the wireless. In those early days it was a novelty, something barely imaginable. Very few people owned a receiving set when the BBC was formed in 1922, and a listener's licence cost 10s. a year. But the father of my friend Maurice Rackow, whom I'd known since we were both ten years old, bought one: a crystal set and coil, a cat's whisker, with the necessary twisted wire to make contact with the sensitive spots in the quartz crystal; and a pair of head-phones. There were no loud-speakers on the market. We would take it in turns to don the headphones, twiddle the cat's whisker and as often as not say 'Stop the clock . . . I think I can hear something.'

Broadcasts of dance bands from outside the BBC's own studios began in 1923 and consisted of programmes of popular dance music played by leading dance bands from exclusive London hotels. I have strong recollections of hearing the Savoy Havannah Band, or the Savoy Orpheans, playing 'When it's Night-time in Italy, it's Wednesday over here' and 'Yes, we have no Bananas'. Eventually, horn loud-speakers were introduced so that families could listen in at the same time. All the same, this new entertainment was so far removed from the world of professional music that no-one grasped its significance at the time.

Meanwhile, I continued to learn about silent films. The orchestras, ranging from a trio to twenty or more musicians, depending on the status of the cinema, provided the atmosphere for the main or feature film, usually lasting about ninety minutes. The remainder of the programme was taken up by a second feature accompanied by a trio, or even just a relief pianist: the Pathé Pictorial News or a cartoon. Programmes were usually changed every three days and ran from Mondays to Wednesdays and from Thursdays to Saturdays, with a completely different film on Sundays. Occasionally a really important film would run for a whole week. The orchestra leader would sit through a showing of the film either in the morning of the day the film was changed or on the previous day, making notes as he watched to indicate the changes of mood: 'mysterious', 'fight', 'party scene', 'military', 'sad' or 'dramatic'. He would also make appropriate cue notes: 'when man seen creeping', 'when men seen fighting', 'when people seen dancing'. Then he would select suitable pieces from his library to fit the scenes.

On the day the film was changed, there would be a call-over for the orchestra. Each member was handed his book. The leader would go through the music calling out the sequence and where each piece was to be started. Often we'd start a section in the middle of a piece that was just right for the scene. Depending on the number of changes required, we might have between twenty and forty different pieces of music on the stand along with the recurring themes: one theme for the romantic young couple, another for the villain. Their music would be perched precariously at extreme ends of the stand while the bulk

20

of the music in the centre had to be played and turned over. There was always one eye on the lookout for the change-of-music cue from the leader, the other eye watching for tempo indications, and one more to read the music and watch for music falling from the stand. And of course, everything had to be played at sight with every change of film. It was all go!

There were many varied types of music, ranging from specially composed pieces to orchestral works by composers like Coleridge-Taylor, Haydn Wood, Eric Coates and Debussy. The range of overtures, symphonies, ballet music, and operatic selections seemed endless, and every Musical Director had his own choice of library. Each time a musician changed his job, he would meet a largely new repertoire. An arranger named Tavan made brilliant operatic selections which could be played by any combination from violin and piano to full orchestra. It was marvellous experience for the pianist to play all the missing cues in these works. A brilliant violinist who lead an orchestra I played in at the age of nineteen, would sometimes decide to substitute a classical work for the fitted music because he preferred it, and people in the audience as well as in the pit might be surprised to hear a violin sonata by Beethoven.

The relief pianist was more limited in his choice of suitable music. Diminished chords were invaluable for scenes of tension and suspense, as well as three famous pieces which remain a legacy of the silent films:

Hearts and Flowers

Hurry No. 1

Misterioso No. 1

Cinemas opened from about 1 pm (sometimes a little earlier) until 11 pm, and usually showed three programmes each day. The

21

musicians would play for half of each programme and rest for the remainder, a playing time of up to five hours. Conditions varied considerably. Larger cinemas had a band-room where they could rest, playing card games such as solo and pontoon. The smaller cinemas were without such facilities, the players having to deposit their hats, coats and instrument cases on the floor of the orchestra pit (as often as not the curtained off part of the cinema below the screen with just enough room to squeeze in an upright piano). The glare of the hooded lights on the music-stands reflecting on the whiteness of the music could be uncomfortable. Glare could be reduced by coloured gelatines, but this also had the effect of distorting the notes, making reading difficult.

Frequently I travelled right across London. I still lived in Shepherds Bush and aged sixteen went to play at Seven Kings beyond Ilford – from one end of London to the other and a distance of between fifteen and twenty miles. Then on to Brockley, beyond New Cross, where I earned £4. 10s. for a seven-day week. I decided to put these hours spent in trains and buses to good use. I joined the library and borrowed books on many different subjects. Armed with a dictionary, I read everything I was able to carry. For having left school at fourteen, I knew only the three Rs and resolved to remedy my educational deficiency by private study.

Having proved to myself that I could do the required work, I was keen to get on and would search the pages of *The Era* (a paper for variety artistes and musicians) for a better job. My youthful appearance and lack of contacts were against me. I remember going to the audition at Brockley; on the same bus, as I learnt later, were three other pianists going to the same audition. A dozen of us sat at the back of the cinema waiting to be called by the leader-violinist. Every pianist had to play the same group of pieces. I was the last to be called, and as I had been listening attentively I had memorized the style of each piece. The difficult one was an overture by Gabriel-Marie called *Le Seigneur de Kermor*. I was offered the job at £4. 10s. a week. The average industrial wage in those days was about £2 per week, so I was definitely on the way up. My hope was to reach a top job, paying £1 a day but this seemed a distant goal – a salary for the top men only in the profession.

The engagement was for seven working days each week; three programme showings each day, and two performances on the Sunday.

22

The first house started at around 1 pm, with the relief pianist and orchestra taking over for the big film between 2.30 and 3 pm. We finished between 10.30 and 11 in the evening and I'd be home about midnight. The only time for piano practice was in the morning; and I still had the same old Parker piano with its dreadful action and jangly tone. But I didn't know that pianos could be any better. All the cinema pianos I played on were of the same quality; even my teacher's left a lot to be desired. It was not until I was nineteen, when I went to a new teacher, that I met a good instrument – the first grand piano I'd encountered. From the moment I began my job in Brockley until I left two years later, I played seven days each week, even on Christmas day, except for the Jewish high holy-days, Rosh Hashanah and Yom Kippur, which my parents insisted on my observing, and which I myself would not have missed whatever the management might have said.

By this time, with Dad, Jack and me working, our standard of living was beginning to improve. My parents decided to improve our home by buying some new furniture. One day my mother said to Jack and me, 'Go into the front room and have a look round.' We went in and on the table was a brand-new gramophone – an HMV table-model with a built-in horn.

We were now able to buy records and hear classical music. Of course there were no long-playing records at the time. One movement of a symphony needed four or five sides of a record for its performance. Caruso, Kreisler, Heifetz, Puccini's *La Bohème*, the Philadelphia Symphony Orchestra playing *Sheherazade* were sounds that brought a new world to me.

We still lived in the same three rooms and kitchen into which we had moved when we first came to Shepherds Bush. One of these was used by my father as his workshop, another room (which was very small) as my parents' bedroom and the third was our front room, or as it was sometimes called the parlour. Jack and I had no bedroom of our own and we slept in this front room sharing a sofa which we opened out each night and closed up each morning. Not a very comfortable bed for two growing young men. I always seemed to be lying on the hard wooden frame! Then we collectively made a momentous decision to buy our own house. Obtaining a building society mortgage, we became the proud owners of a house in Melrose Terrace, Shepherds Bush. We moved into new and spacious premises: a whole house, with a whole bedroom for Jack and myself and a whole bed each. And of course still retaining our Parker piano!

At nineteen I was making good progress on the piano and was able to play Chopin, Beethoven and other classical composers. My brother was studying privately with Rowsby Woof from the Royal Academy of Music, and one day, having accompanied Jack in one of his solos, I spoke to his teacher about a possible tutor for myself. He recommended an Academy colleague, John Pauer, son of a world famous pianist Max Pauer, and I took lessons from him, learning the correct use of the pedals, not as loud or soft pedals but as a means of aiding musical phrasing and expression.

Pauer wanted me to sit for a scholarship, which he was sure I'd get. However, it would mean having to give up playing in cinemas and concentrating on full-time academic study, and after much discussion at home, we decided it would be too expensive. Many times since I've wondered what direction my career would have taken had I gained a scholarship which would have involved the study of harmony, counterpoint and theory. It may seem strange to present day classical musicians, but when I was young the average musician knew nothing of these subjects, and I myself was under the impression that the great composers wrote naturally simply because they were great! Most of my contemporaries came from a similar background to myself: offspring of Jewish immigrants whose hope was that their sons would not be tailors or shoe repairers. One learnt the piano or the violin and became a competent instrumentalist. To paraphrase a Yiddish saying: 'From where should they know from such things like harmony?' The Royal College of Music and the Royal Academy of Music were places where wealthy people sent their children to learn the piano. 'Harmony – what sort of a thing is that!'

It was soon after we had moved into our new house that I became friends with a young Scottish cellist named David Greenbaum. He was studying at the Royal College of Music. Eventually, to escape from living with an unpleasant uncle, he came to live with us. He would often bring home music and with Jack on the violin I have happy memories of our getting to know the Schubert, Arensky and Beethoven trios from the college library which he, Jack and I would sight-read.

David also introduced me to a broadcasting studio. A brilliant cellist, he had been invited by the BBC (which had recently changed its name from the British Broadcasting Company to the British Broadcasting Corporation) to broadcast a cello sonata. He agreed, but only if I were allowed to accompany him. And so it was that the two of us, both extremely young, went to 2LO studio in Savoy Hill off the Strand, the first broadcasting studio in the country, to perform to the world – or at least that part of it possessing receiver sets. The studio was a smallish room containing a grand piano (the best instrument I had ever played on), a music stand and microphone. When the little red light on the wall lit up, we duly played and gave of our best. This would have been about 1927 or 1928 – a long, long time ago in the history of radio.

I'd been working with John Pauer for about a year when my mother became ill and neurotic, and the domestic scene began to deteriorate. My parents quarrelled a great deal and relations became strained. Eventually my father inexplicably left the household, leaving me as the provider and supporter. My brother, who had married at an early age, lived upstairs with his wife Rosie, but of course he had his own responsibilities to his new family. So, at the age of nineteen, I became head of the household and said farewell to my studies. Another of my deep regrets.

I had been playing in cinema orchestras of various kinds since I was fourteen-and-a-half years of age and was beginning to know more musicians and was also becoming known in that world. I thought that was how most of my future life would be spent – as a pianist in cinema orchestras, possibly even becoming a conductor. It seemed a secure profession. After all, there would always be films and they would always need musical accompaniment, whether from a trio or a large orchestra. The work was always interesting for me, and I enjoyed meeting more and more new music, particularly in the musical interludes where the orchestra would be featured and play a whole piece of music right through instead of playing only a part of it to suit a particular scene.

Perhaps a word or two here regarding these 'musical interludes' would not be out of place. Usually they were performed at the end of one of the feature films and the leader, who was invariably a violinist, would mount a small platform (sometimes a box or an empty beer crate) and face the audience, who could only see his head and shoulders. The rest of him, like the orchestra, would be hidden by the orchestral curtain. When the spotlight shone on him, he would lead his orchestra of whatever size, in a spirited performance of an overture like *Poet and Peasant*, *Raymond* or *William Tell*, or possibly play solos such as Toselli's *Serenade*, *In a Monastery Garden* or *In a Persian Market*.

It must be emphasized and remembered that in the days before radio, and even during its early days, the vast majority of the public literally never heard any music and so they were usually very attentive and appreciative. The leaders of these orchestras were often local celebrities. I remember in one of my earlier engagements (I was about seventeen), the leader asking me to play some solos instead of the usual orchestral item, and so a scratchy slide was shown on the screen with the message, 'Musical Interlude. Piano Solo by Louis Mordish, who will play *Gnomenreigen* by Liszt'. On another occasion, just to show how versatile I was expected to be, I played Billy Mayerl's *Jazz Master* – both of which were played of course out of sight of the audience as I was behind the curtain, though with the white spotlight pointing to where my head and shoulders would have been had I been standing up.

In later years, as cinemas moved into the 'super cinema' class and orchestras became correspondingly larger, these interludes became featured parts of the programme. I recall hearing Louis Levy and his Orchestra, nattily attired in red jackets, sitting in semi-concert fashion on the stage of the Shepherds Bush Pavilion, then one of London's largest cinemas, giving a very exciting performance of the overture *Zampa*. Some of the more adventurous of the smaller cinemas with stages would also have a special 'live show' on Friday evening, usually called 'Novelty Night'. Would-be up-and-coming acts appeared and did their turn for about 7s. 6d. hoping to be seen by agents and get more bookings. A comedian, an instrumentalist or a vocalist would be drawn in by the management to tempt the public into the cinema on the worst day of the week for business – payday – when everyone went out to do their shopping.

With the growing popularity of dance tunes, publishers began to bring out printed orchestrations so that orchestras as well as dance bands would be able to play their songs. These often included parts for such instruments as horns, cellos and violas. The normal orchestra would contain a high proportion of violins playing the melody supported by the first trumpet player. There were no microphones or loud-speakers in theatres or cinemas and so people at the back of the

26

hall had difficulty in hearing the music, especially if the hall was full. Hence the need for a strong melody.

Palais de Dance also became popular in the early 1920s, and more dance bands were beginning to experiment with different line-ups. Whereas in the very early days of jazz one could hear a great deal of improvisation on the part of the players, the dancing public could now be offered carefully written and rehearsed band items. There were people like Debroy Somers, the leader of the famous Savoy Orpheans at the Savoy Hotel, who made rhythmic arrangements for dance bands with pieces like the *Scottish Medley*, the *Irish Medley*, and the *Christmas Medley*, all being selections of well-known tunes played in the same strict dance tempo, and Eddie Lange in America, who arranged rhythmic paraphrases of *Il Trovatore*, *Naila Waltz* (in 4/4 time!), *Russian Fantasy* and a host of others all trying to get away from the song-chorus type of number and bring something of a higher cultural level into the dance-music world. The world of rhythm-music was an explosive one; new styles, new ideas, new forms of jazz were continually coming to the fore. Because of the rapid improvement of the wireless, and its consequent impact on a new listening public, hitherto unknown performers and entertainers were becoming nationally known household names. One of the greatest revolutions in popular music was the introduction of microphones and loud-speakers into the world of entertainment.

Being somewhat highbrow in my tastes, I was only slightly interested in the development of dance music, preferring to earn my living playing straight music in cinema orchestras rather than playing four-beats-to-the-bar dance music in the Palais. I was aware of the changes from the old ragtime rhythm, the one-step, the foxtrot, the black bottom, the blues but to me they were all variations on the basic four-beats-to-the-bar whether fast, medium or slow tempo. Possibly my standards were wrong, but I could not stand the thought that one day I might have to earn my living playing in a Palais band with every piece of music other than waltzes having the same monotonous four beats to every bar for a whole evening, every evening.

Though some people in the mid-twenties saw the developments taking place in the world of sound-film recording as novelties rather than a threat to the silent film, the phenomenal success of *The Jazz Singer* in 1927 showed that this new-fangled novelty called 'talkies' had arrived to stay. Musicians began to realize that their whole profession was threatened. Orchestras would no longer be required, as one studio orchestra per film would provide enough music for the whole world's showing of that film. Apprehension was everywhere as cinemas were wired-up for talkies and began to dispense with orchestras. Like the silent-film stars thrown out of work because their voices were unsuitable for sound recording, thousands of musicians all over the country were suddenly with no prospect of finding another job.

I was very lucky. Though my cinema was wired up, I was offered a job in another which was not yet ready for the new medium. I was out of work for a few weeks only – although with no dole it did not seem brief at the time. I was thrilled one day to receive a phone call from the musical supervisor of a large cinema circuit called Provincial Cinematograph Theatres asking whether I'd be interested in a job at the Marlborough Cinema in Holloway, North London, where the policy was to show one talkie film and one silent film, for which the orchestra would play each programme. This would continue until there were no more silent films. I was surprised that he knew of me and jumped at the chance, £6 per week, with the prospect of several months work.

The Marlborough was a music hall which had been converted into a cinema. In addition to playing for the film, the orchestra was required to provide a musical interlude. The conductor, a portly sluggish man whose musical ability left much to be desired, would say to me while his podgy arms were held aloft before he gave his ponderous down-beat, 'Jazz it up son, jazz it up' – which I dutifully did!

After some months at the Marlborough, which had now become part of the giant Gaumont-British circuit, I was transferred to the Broadway, Stratford, in East London, where there was an orchestra of sixteen – the largest I'd ever played in. Here again we performed both for the remaining silent films and also for variety acts now being introduced as part of the regular programme.

It was a novel mixture. While some of the specially written film music and the standard light orchestral works were very well scored, with parts for the woodwind and french horns, the variety-act music left much to be desired. And so I was able to study the more unusual orchestral parts at the same time as I was learning to play routines such as: 'The last four bars for intro – cut to verse – play three choruses – two vocal and one for dance – third chorus play 'stop' – repeat the last four bars three times, the third in half tempo and then chord to finish – repeat and keep repeating last eight bars for 'tabs' till artiste off.' But what experience! What with my original classical piano study, playing for silent films and variety, and even the occasional dance-gig, I was rapidly developing a wide acquaintance with many different types of music.

When I was about sixteen, I met an orchestral and band leader through an advertisement in *The Era*. He was a middle-aged Dutchman named Victor Vorzanger and, as I learnt later, a great character. In his early days he had been famous for his 'Blue Hussars' orchestra which played on the bandstands at seaside resorts. But by the time I met him he had entered the dance-band world and was leader of a band in a London Palais. He liked the way I played, and in the following years frequently gave me dates whenever I could fit them in with my regular job. These would usually be society functions. A small orchestra would very discretely perform during the dinner and later be augmented with saxes, brass and rhythm for the dance. Victor was also very well known for his gypsy orchestra and many was the time I donned one of his old Blue Hussar uniforms. These looked like a cross between the garb of a military bandsman and an old-fashioned circus lion-tamer with epaulettes, gigantic stiff cuffs and heavy gold stripes across the chest.

My first engagement was at an end-of-term garden party at a big private school. We were duly met at the country station by a Lea-Francis car, the poshest car I had ever been in. After we'd changed into our gypsy uniforms, we were escorted on to the lawn where an upright piano had been placed. It was a beautifully sunny afternoon and I was looking forward to an enjoyable programme in the open air. I asked Victor for the music.

'Music,' he replied, 'there's no music. Gypsies don't play from music. And by the way,' he added, looking at the rest of us, 'If anyone here speaks one word of English, I will personally kill him! Remember, you're all foreign!' I asked what we were going to play. 'Don't worry,' he said, 'Just keep vamping and follow me.'

I was petrified, but carried on busking all the same! And so we played, Victor standing right next to me, scratching away on his violin with the bow hairs flying out, smiling away at the people gathering around. The other musicians scraped and scratched, wading through pieces like *The Blue Danube* and *Black Eyes* in an inspired gypsy way. Near us stood a couple of dear old ladies listening intently. My face was red with embarrassment and I was hoping the ground would open up and swallow me. I felt so ashamed of my busking, but we must have sounded well for I heard one of them say to the other: 'These gypsy musicians are wonderful. They play with such fire and passion.' At which remark, we all scratched and scraped and banged away with greater enthusiasm.

Many cinemas were closed on Sundays, because a large percentage of box-office takings had, by law, to be given to charity. Instead, many theatres and music halls ran special concerts for the general public which were sponsored by 'Sunday League Concerts for the People'. Victor's orchestra often played for these concerts. The programmes were usually made up by a small orchestra playing popular pieces such as the *Light Cavalry Overture, Bells across the Meadows*, a cello or trumpet solo, male and female vocalists singing solos and duets, and a comedian. Programmes were printed with the names of all the artistes and orchestral musicians on the front page, and I distinctly remember one programme with the words in very small print under the other names: 'Arthur Askey, comedian'.

We were always on stage, and on one occasion the orchestra had gone down so well that the audience were applauding and clamouring for more. But we had exhausted all our repertoire, including the encores. There was literally nothing else we could play. Victor walked to the footlights. 'In response to your very kind applause,' he said when the clapping had subsided, 'I would like to play for you my latest composition. While strolling through the woods one day, I heard some birds singing, and I was so inspired that I went straight home and wrote this piece which I shall now play for you.'

The rest of us looked at each other in consternation. What was he going to play? Casually, he strolled over to the piano and while he was making great work of tuning his violin, turned his back to the audience and told me to keep vamping in A. Then, half turning to the drummer he said, 'When I nod to you, give me an oom-pah beat getting faster and louder.' He then faced the audience and began to play, making weird and wonderful bird-whistling effects playing harmonics, then started to scratch out some sort of tune using a great deal of open E and A strings while I vamped dutifully – trying at the same time to look equally inspired. After the composition had taken some sort of shape, he gave the pre-arranged nod, the drummer joined in with his oom-pah rhythm and the rest of the orchestra, capturing the mood and the spirit then joined in, all improvising in the key of A major. The result was extraordinary but a fantastic success.

On yet another occasion I had to arrive late at a society function, and Victor agreed to leave a uniform out for me with the butler. When I tried on the jacket, I was horrified: it reached down to my knees and the sleeves were six inches too long. However, I just had to wear it. From the ballroom where I heard a piano playing Wagner's 'Magic Fire Music' from *Die Valkyrie*. I saw a group of very elegant young ladies standing round a piano at the far end of the room. As I entered, trying to be as unobtrusive as possible, the pianist stopped playing and the whole company stared at me as I went along my embarrassed way. My discomfort was only increased when I saw the pianist was Ivor Novello!

As a teenager I had virtually no social life at all. I spent the mornings practising the piano and the rest of the day in the cinema. However, when I went to the Rotherhithe Hippodrome (another of the many music halls which had been converted into a cinema) I had Sundays off. Socially, I did not know what to do with myself. I did not belong to any youth club, and the only one I knew of was associated with a synagogue. But I was much too shy and inhibited to go there on my own and try to make friends.

By this time, my friend Maurice's father owned a car, a black Ford saloon. As Maurice had learnt to drive, he automatically became the chauffeur any time a member of his family wanted to go anywhere. It was still a comparatively rare thing for an ordinary middle-class person to own a car and I knew no-one else who possessed one. To be able to go for a ride in one's own car indicated a standard of living to be envied. Many times, visiting his house on Sunday, I secretly hoped that someone would say 'It's a fine day, let's go for a drive', and that I would be included in the general invitation. On the occasions when I did go for a ride with the family, I enjoyed every moment and savoured to the full the sense of privilege in being able to be in a car instead of sitting in a bus.

Some time later, Maurice, who had become a medical student, joined the synagogue youth club. I also went occasionally and came in contact with Maurice's new circle of friends: young men and women who seemed so intelligent and full of confidence that when anyone spoke to me I blushed – a distressing characteristic that I have never quite outgrown. Having no female relatives of any kind other than my mother, I knew little about the opposite sex. My parents never at any time spoke to me or to my brother about the facts of life. This was a taboo subject, and never discussed. Amongst the musicians with whom I worked the level of the remarks made were generally of a ribald and coarse nature. On the rare occasions when it became a more serious topic of conversation I discovered that most young men were either as ignorant as I was concerning the subject or had grossly distorted views. During social encounters with the daughters of friends, I found myself getting somewhat tongue-tied and could never talk to them without blushing.

My mother's attitude was that of her generation: a respectable Jewish man and girl would meet, go out together a few times and, if they liked each other enough, get engaged and marry after a period of six months to a year. Well-meaning friends tried to arrange for me to meet pretty Jewish girls at tea parties. After all, I was now in my twenties: time for a nice Jewish boy to settle down. In those days Jewish mothers were horrified at the thought that their sons would marry out of the faith: to marry a gentile girl was the absolute nadir. Although many young men made the acquaintance of non-Jewish girls at dances it was unheard of to invite them back to meet the family. Indeed, on one occasion when a girl whom I had met at a friend's house phoned me, my mother nearly went into hysterics at the very thought that this girl might be the one to lead me astray from the path of my ancestors. Horror of horrors!

Pianist-composer

I think I am correct in saying that Jewish musicians at this time knew little about organs, because they were never used in the orthodox synagogues and were seen as Christian instruments. So I well remember my first encounter with a cinema organ at Stratford Broadway Cinema. It was a two-manual Wurlitzer, then regarded as a wonderful innovation. The original organist, Archie Parkhouse, was a very good showman, if not a very good player. He was later replaced by Lloyd Thomas, whom I immediately recognized as an excellent musician. There was a piano in the music-library room, and as I had been appointed official orchestral librarian (for an extra 10s. a week) I was able to play it whenever I wished. I knew Lloyd to be a polished performer, and we often had stimulating talks about piano music.

On one occasion I was playing a Chopin étude between performances when there was a knock on the door and one of the variety artistes came in. He was a middle-aged man and I was about twenty-two. 'I hope you don't mind me saying it,' he said, 'but you know, you'll never get anywhere with that sort of stuff. If you want to please the public, you've got to give 'em tunes, son, tunes.' (He pronounced the word as 'chunes'.) Not exactly the right sort of encouragement for a serious-minded young pianist. I was very hurt at the time. But somehow, looking back at the world of entertainment over the years, I think he was right.

This was the beginning of the big band era. The line-up of such bands varied considerably. Henry Hall with his BBC Dance Band created a minor sensation when he introduced an oboe into his orchestra. Jack Hylton retained violins, but more or less standardized the form by having larger brass and saxophone sections. He was also one of the first to present a dance band as a stage show-band as distinct from one which just played for dancing in a palais. As our own cinema orchestra was not a dance band as such, one of the higher-ups decided to present us on stage in costume, as this was the current fashion.

We were transformed from a cinema orchestra into a Spanish ensemble, and our conductor, Tom Priddy, converted into Don Predo. For these stage presentations we were all given so-called Spanish costumes: different coloured breeches and stockings, jackets in weird and assorted styles and certainly never from anywhere near Spain. With our kerchiefs on our heads, we must have looked like a bunch of bewildered and unhappy pirates. We played the *1812 Overture*, and selections from *The Gypsy Princess* and current musical comedies, with a vocalist to supply appropriate colour to the songs. I don't know where the Spanish element came in, but the audience loved it.

Feeling more secure financially, I decided to buy a second-hand car. I was about twenty-three, and like all young men felt the urge to be fashionable. In those days driving tests did not exist. Anyone who wanted to drive just got into a car and learnt as they went along. One of the violinists in the orchestra offered to give me lessons. When I answered an advertisement in the *Evening Standard* for a Rover open-air tourer (today it would be called a convertible), my friend came with me as the expert and approved of it. I became the proud owner of my first car at the cost of £18 cash. I can still recall the number, KO18. My friend drove it home, and after explaining a few things such as gears and double declutching, allowed me to drive it. We decided to go to work in it on Monday for the change-of-variety-act rehearsals.

On the great day I took the wheel with my friend sitting beside me and drove most of the way from Shepherds Bush to Stratford, from the West of London to the East, going through Oxford Street, the West End, the City, the East End and arriving at the theatre in style to find the whole orchestra lined up in two facing rows, waving and cheering while I drove triumphantly between.

After that I drove regularly to and from the cinema. Then one evening I decided to surprise my mother, who had not yet seen our show. I would go home in my Spanish costume. One of the musicians in the orchestra, who had a great sense of humour (or so he thought) always insisted that we wore appropriate make-up, and on this special occasion he made up my face vividly and completed it with a fierce-looking moustache and sideboards. I drove off in my costume and as it was a warm summer evening, the hood of the car was down. Travelling along the Strand I somehow stalled the engine. As there was no self-starter to the car, I had to rely on the starting handle. I clambered out, the starter in my hand, when a policeman who had been on traffic control approached to find out why I had stopped, thereby causing a build-up of traffic. In no time at all a large group gathered to stare at this spectacle. I shall never forget the policeman's expression when he saw me in my Spanish costume with my fierce painted moustache, flourishing a starter handle in my hand.

Hotel and restaurant orchestras were very much a popular institution. In London there were the famous Lyons Corner Houses at Oxford Street, The Strand and Coventry Street. These huge restaurants on several floors each had a large orchestra led by famous violinists such as Albert Sandler. The high spot of many people's weekend would be a visit to one of these Corner Houses to hear the orchestra while eating a meal of tea, roll, butter and pastries brought to them by Nippies – waitresses in neat black uniform with white aprons and head-bands. When Albert Sandler, who was one of the early BBC Grand Hotel leaders, left the firm of Lyons Corner Houses to go the Hyde Park Hotel, it was front-page news. De Groot at the Piccadilly Hotel was another famous hotel orchestra leader who was often in the headlines.

Smaller restaurants in the big department stores and teashops in the West End and in the larger provincial towns had a trio or quartet playing during meals. Such music provided a pleasant atmosphere and a personal link between customers and café management. Many brilliant instrumentalists earned their living playing in such orchestras, not least Alfredo Campoli, who in later years became a famous concert violinist, and Albert Sammons, who also became one of England's outstanding recitalists.

Grand Hotel, in which the Palm Court Orchestra played popular and easy to listen to middle-of-the-road music such as Viennese waltzes, musical comedy and light operatic selections, was one of the longest running and most popular of radio light music programmes. It originally started with the live broadcasting from the Grand Hotel, Eastbourne, under the leadership of Leslie Jeffries. The programme was later transferred to the studios, maintaining the restaurant atmosphere by the discreet sounds of crockery being manipulated in the background. This programme ran for over forty years before being disbanded in the 1970s by the BBC, only to be revived after a lapse of several years.

From time to time variety acts at the Stratford Broadway Cinema included troupes of dancing girls such as The Sherman Fisher Girls and The Betty Hobbs Eight, who always wore colourful bright stage costumes which were invariably one-piece dresses, sometimes with the addition of a bolero style of jacket. One day there was a sensation when a troupe of girls appeared on stage in costumes which revealed a bare midriff of about two inches. It was the first time that any of us had seen anything so daring and much was the talking and expressions of opinion – no doubt accompanied by solemn shaking of the head – among the members of the public. Of course, over the years costumes have shrunk more until there is more midriff than coverage. Today the situation is quite the reverse.

We began to hear rumours of a possible change of conductor. For whatever reason, perhaps because some members of the orchestra addressed him as Tom instead of Mr Priddy and thereby decreased the discipline, the musical management decided to make a change. We heard that a man named Van Dam was going to take over. He was known as a strict disciplinarian who did not tolerate passengers in an orchestra. Those in the know warned us that we could all expect to be sacked or transferred when he took over.

There was a good deal of apprehension for weeks beforehand, and on the very first Monday morning rehearsal, we were all sitting in our places in good time, waiting for the new Musical Director. A man of about twenty-nine or so entered the pit, mounted the conductor's rostrum. Few of us had ever seen him. He was thin and wore glasses with very thick lenses. He tapped the music stand with his baton for attention and, glancing from side to side, covered every member with a stare. 'Before we start rehearsing,' he said, 'I'd like to make one or two things absolutely clear. I'm the conductor of this orchestra and things are going to be done my way. I understand that some members are not pleased at my being here, so if they feel they won't be happy with me – they can go.' What a way to start! Within a few weeks, he got many members of the orchestra transferred to other cinemas and brought in men from his former orchestras. I was one of the few who remained. He obviously liked my work and much to everybody's amazement we eventually became very good friends. Our friendship extended beyond professional circles to our families. We frequently visited each other's homes and even holidayed in the South of France on one occasion after the War. This friendship only ended with Van Dam's death in 1973.

In these early days of talkies it was not unusual for the sound on films to get lost or distorted. It was a normal thing for the larger cinemas to have a sound engineer whose sole function was to sit at the back of the cinema and twiddle the sound knobs to regulate the volume, and to be prepared to deal with a breakdown in the sound. The musical advisor to the firm decided that in the event of the film and sound breaking down, music should be used to keep the audience entertained. As non-synch records and panatropes (large gramophone records) were not yet standard in cinemas, the job of supplying this music was to be the responsibility of the organist. Large cinemas employed two organists: the solo organist who only played interludes (the organ rising from the pit was still a novelty), and his assistant, who had to be on duty ready to fill in during a film breakdown.

There were two such organists at the Stratford Broadway Cinema: Lloyd Thomas and his assistant. Against my will I was forced to take an interest in it as the musical advisor decided that in the interests of economy, the firm would dispense with second organists and the orchestra pianists would take over their function. Knowing absolutely nothing at all about the subject, I asked Lloyd to explain what the knobs and tabs were for. For some months, in addition to playing the piano in the orchestra, I stood by, though the only organ playing I did was to play the National Anthem at the end of the day's programme. For this I had to wait until eleven o'clock each night while the rest of the orchestra left after the last stage show. But as I received an extra £1 per week for this, I couldn't complain. These were the years of high unemployment following the 1929 Wall Street crash, the world slump and the introduction of talkies. No musician was in a position to argue with his employer. He was lucky to be working. I was getting £6 as pianist, £1 as stand-by organist and 10s. as librarian.

Eventually Van Dam left the firm to go as Musical Director to the newest and greatest cinema in Europe, the Trocadero at the Elephant and Castle. This most luxurious theatre seated about 4,000 people and offered the public two feature films as well as a stage show and orchestra. There was also the legendary Quentin Maclean, undoubtedly the greatest of all theatre organists, at the largest Wurlitzer organ in England, plus news films and interest films. The four-hour programmes cost sixpence.

Van Dam asked me to go with him as his pianist. I could get more money at the Trocadero, and could also take organ lessons from Quentin Maclean. Van Dam pointed out that the organ was the instrument of the future and said I'd be foolish not to take advantage of such an opportunity. I turned down his invitation with the excuse that his job was with a new firm, the Hyams Brothers, and might not last whereas I had been with the Gaumont British firm for some years and was reasonably sure of some sort of security while they were still in business. Also, still not being very enthusiastic about the cinema organ, I said – and how well I remember those words – 'I'd much rather earn my bread and butter playing a legitimate musical instrument than by playing a box of tricks.' So I continued for another year with this rather hum-drum job, until the musical advisor to the firm asked me to go to the Kit-Kat Restaurant, which they also controlled, and play with the restaurant orchestra under the leadership of Harold Sandler, brother of the great Albert. As it would be for the same firm I agreed, thinking it would make a change from an uninspiring routine. There were several pianists sent along for an audition and I was selected.

This new job was quite different, and opened up for me yet another world of light music. We played during lunch and dinner, wearing gypsy-type blouses, and I learnt a good deal about the café style of playing and its own type of repertoire from Harold Sandler, who was superb. On Sundays we supplied the relief band music for dancing, specializing in tangos. The Kit-Kat was one of the famous restaurants of the early 30s and the two resident dance bands were the Roy Fox and Joe Loss Orchestras. It was altogether different from playing in a cinema for variety acts and stage shows, and being a stand-by organist.

Van Dam and I kept in touch. He was very keen on his own stage presentations with his orchestra and knowing that I could write and arrange (something we had often discussed when he was at the Broadway Cinema), he asked me to make some arrangements. I can still recall *Remember my forgotten man* (a musical follow-up to the great song of the 30s depression, *Buddy, can you spare a dime*) and a rhythmic-operatic selection which included the Barcarolle from Offenbach's *Tales of Hoffman*.

New super cinemas were still being built in the 30s, despite the depression. One of these, the Commodore at Hammersmith, was known nationally, and its orchestra had become famous through their popular programmes transmitted every Saturday morning. The conductor, Joseph Muscant, was reputed to be very difficult to please musically, and because of his fame, virtually unapproachable. When I got to know him later, I felt this inapproachability was a defence complex against a musical inferiority.

His pianist until about two years previously had been Sidney Torch, who left in order to become pianist in the orchestra at yet another super cinema, the Regal at Marble Arch, where he later became the organist. Since Torch's departure, quite a number of well-known players had taken his place but none of them lasted longer than a few months at the most. Several of my friends suggested that I apply for the job but my response was invariably negative. The orchestra's prestige was extremely high and I had heard glowing accounts of the abilities of these pianists. There would be little chance for me.

One week, the Commodore Orchestra appeared as a special attraction at the Trocadero Cinema where Van Dam was also presenting his own orchestra. One of the items played by Van (as he was always called) was my *Rhythmic Operatic Selection*. Joseph Muscant was so impressed that he sent a message via Van asking to see me. Van had obviously been talking to him, because when I called at Muscant's dressing room, I was dumbfounded. He offered me the job as pianist in the famous Commodore Orchestra, and he'd never even heard me play. As I was still playing at the Kit-Kat Restaurant, the move meant a great deal professionally. Then and there, he wrote a letter confirming my engagement to start in a fortnight at the salary of £8 10s. weekly plus 5s. for each broadcast. As the national average wage was no more than £2 a week this was a princely sum. In addition to the weekly broadcast, there were also regular recording sessions for labels like Regal-Zonophone, which retailed at 1s. 6d. each. I was over the moon.

I stayed with the Commodore Orchestra for two years, until Joseph Muscant's contract expired. During this period, in addition to our theatre work of accompanying the stage shows, our regular

39

broadcasts took up a fair amount of time each evening. We rehearsed in the band-room, where space was limited. There was not enough room for a piano and I think the rehearsals were as much for Joe Muscant as they were for the players. He was very fond of medleys and pot-pourris and would string together many pieces by the same composer or on a common theme. So we would have the *Grieg Medley*, the *Schubert Medley*, the *Victor Herbert Medley* plus *Musical Comedy Medley*, *Viennese Waltz Medley* or a *March Medley*. My job was to write all the connecting links between items so that each medley became one long unbroken piece of music lasting from fifteen to twenty minutes. I was also expected to play solos as required by the music. In the *Grieg Medley* I had to play the first movement of the Piano Concerto, including the full cadenza, and in the *Liszt Medley*, the cadenza of the Second Hungarian Rhapsody.

On one occasion, Joe (as we called him behind his back) said he wanted me to play Dohnány's arrangement of the *Naila Waltz* by Delibes at a concert in three weeks time. There was no point arguing I didn't know it; the job was too precious. I bought a copy and practised like mad. It is a difficult virtuoso work. When the moment came in the programme for the solo, I was so nervous that although I was playing, I felt it was somebody else, as if I could have detached myself and watched this person. It was the first time I had actually broadcast such a difficult piece. Not like the Grieg or Liszt concertos, which were led into and followed by the orchestra, but an item completely on its own. Because of my nervousness, I think I played it very fast, knocking about 45 seconds off the usual timing. But I didn't get the sack. Every performance on radio or in the recording world was live and everything had to be right, from the beginning to the end. The Commodore Gold Medal Orchestra made many records while I was with them, including *In a Persian Market* and *In a Monastery Garden* and one recording which was a selection from *Die Fledermaus*, the first time I had been asked to arrange and orchestrate music for a commercial recording. I think the Commodore Orchestra was so successful because the acoustics in the theatre restaurant which was used as our broadcasting studio were exceptionally good.

I also recorded a novelty piano solo called *The Knave of Diamonds*, another nerve-racking experience. This took place on the Commodore stage with the orchestra at one end and myself at the piano at the other end to accommodate a new technique in recording whereby two microphones were used. As recordings were still being made on wax, no time could be wasted. As soon as the red warning light went on, Joe Muscant gave the down-beat and I began the number with a solo run from the top of the piano. The piece ended with another long solo run – this time from the bottom to the top of the instrument and throughout the recording of the piece, which was quite tricky to play, I was worried about fluffing this last run, though everything went off well. I was given a copy of the record and often used it when I became an organist. As a novelty presentation in one of my organ interludes, I would have it played over the cinema sound-speaker system while I accompanied on the organ, in reality accompanying myself. Like so many other things, this record disappeared during the War. I was without a copy until someone at an organ society concert where I was playing told me he still had a record of this item.

Another new experience was the promotion by music publishers of their latest popular songs and light music by plugging. They employed men whose task was to contact broadcasting artistes, in order to acquaint them with their latest publications and persuade them to include these pieces in their programmes. As each broadcast performance of any piece of music earned a royalty fee for the publisher, it was obviously highly desirable that friendly relations should be developed between the artiste and the plugger, whose job depended on the success of his contacts with performers.

And so a system developed whereby the pluggers would do the rounds, entertaining artistes from dance-band leaders and conductors of light orchestras to vocalists and broadcasting organists. In the course of friendly discussions and gossip over a pint of beer, the plugger would mention the title of the number he was working on and offer a copy. Most artistes were too conscientious to perform numbers they did not honestly care for. But so intense was the competition between publishers that, quite openly, some of the pluggers began to offer cash or presents to potential performers for the inclusion of their publication in broadcast programmes. Quite a number of performers made a sizeable addition to their broadcast fee by playing medleys of popular tunes, each of which carried a plugging fee. Indeed, the system became so open and widespread that the BBC had to take drastic steps to end the practice.

One song-promoter was Frank Rubens. He was the Professional Department Manager of Feldmans, one of the biggest of the old-time publishing houses in the field of popular songs, and a very experienced man in the world of entertainment. He had heard Van Dam and his orchestra playing some of my arrangements made for his stage presentations, including the *Operatic Rhythmic Selection* in which I had joined the ranks of arrangers who were trying to get away from the ordinary song-type of score. He must have been impressed because he asked to see me. He amazed me by saying that he liked what he had heard of my work and wanted me to do an arrangement for Jack Hylton's Band of a popular song about a lamplighter. I jumped at the opportunity, and when Frank told me the arrangements had to be ready and in the recording studio by 10 o'clock the following morning, I agreed, even though I knew it meant sitting up all night. I started writing late that evening, having finished the day's playing at the Commodore, and worked away, fortified by frequent cups of coffee. My arranging was done without a score, and because of the lateness of the hour, I dared not use the piano to help work out various passages. The whole thing was a dreadful battle against time – and the nearby church clock.

The following morning it was practically complete. Not wishing to be late for this wonderful occasion – my very first specially commissioned arrangement for the great Jack Hylton – I took a taxi and arrived bleary eyed at the studio. I sat in the corner of the very large room, finishing the parts and watched by a curious Peter Yorke, Jack's principal arranger. I was extremely nervous when it was time for my arrangement to be tried. I expected my all-night session to result in a dreadful cacophony of wrong notes and wrong transpositions, but everything turned out well. It was not a great arrangement, but obviously good enough to be issued as a commercial recording.

At this time I was also working on a suite for orchestra called *A Legend of the Woods* in three movements: 'Elfin Ballet', 'By the Haunted Mere' and 'Nightfall – Ride of the Witches'. Being unaware of such a thing as a score, I did it the hard way. As with all my compositions and arrangements up to this time I headed each separate sheet of manuscript paper with the name of an instrument

– flute, oboe, clarinet, violin, trumpet – then spread the pages over the table and wrote on each individual part, orchestrating the piece of music as I went along. The writing took me a very long time as I continually had to inspect, check and compare each part as I wrote. There was no thought of publication in my mind when I knew so little about full-scale orchestration. I wrote because I felt like it and hoped vaguely that somehow in the future, I might be able to hear it played.

When it was completed, I persuaded some of the musicians in the orchestra to get together and play excerpts. They were very complimentary. One of them, Charlie Jones the flautist, who was due to leave the Commodore orchestra to take up an appointment with the BBC Theatre Orchestra, suggested I send the work to the orchestra's conductor, Stanford Robinson. I had actually accompanied Charlie at his audition for that particular engagement some time previously. When I pointed out that it would be difficult for a new work to be read by a conductor from the orchestral parts, the magic word 'score' was mentioned. One of the musicians said I should send the score and not worry just yet about the parts. It was then that I realized what an almost impossible task I had been attempting. So a new world had opened up for me. Having learnt what a score was and after studying some miniature scores, I set to work compiling a score from the individual orchestral parts: definitely the wrong way round.

Eventually it was completed and sent to Stanford Robinson. I was thrilled when, some weeks later, I received a letter saying how much he'd liked it and had decided to include the suite in a forthcoming broadcast. Would I care to come along to the rehearsal on the day?

I could barely wait for the great day to arrive. Accompanied by my friend David Greenbaum, I duly went to the old St George's Hall which was used as the broadcasting studio and was next to the old Queen's Hall (both buildings were destroyed during the Second World War). We sat in the front row of the empty concert hall, looking up at the orchestra. When Stanford Robinson arrived we chatted for a couple of minutes. He said he was going to rehearse the programme in sequence.

It was the first time I had attended the rehearsal of such a large orchestra. I sat through the rehearsal in a state of amazed disbelief. Until then I had only visualized the sounds in my mind. Did I write that, I kept thinking? Yet it all sounded correct; not at all like a home-made piece of music. At the end of the rehearsal of my suite

43

the members of the orchestra applauded. That particular performance was the very first time I had heard a large orchestra playing one of my compositions. It was a wonderful feeling.

After that I sent the same work to the different BBC orchestras and was fortunate and gratified to hear it performed by practically every BBC light orchestra in the different regions, by such conductors as Guy Warrack, Jack Leon, Charles Shadwell, Frank Cantell and Paul Fenoulhet. And flushed with its continuing success, I tried to get the suite published. Van Lier, head of Keith Prowse, heard me play it for him but said very kindly, 'You know, it's very difficult to get biggish works like this played even though you have had BBC performances of it and it costs a lot of money to print and produce. If you want to write music for publishing, why don't you write a diddle-te-tum-te-tum-te type of piece which lots of small orchestras can play.' Disillusioned, I took his advice and concocted a little diddle-te-tum-te-tum-te number called *The Marionette and the Wooden Soldier* (those were the days when many pieces of light music had very fanciful titles). Van Lier liked it. It became my first published number, beautifully printed on beautiful quality paper with a beautiful colour drawing on the cover, beautifully designed and produced and ready for the public at the beautiful price of 2*s*. Moreover, it opened doors to other publishing houses. Before long I was writing light numbers with considerable success. However, as people felt that one composer could not possibly write in a number of styles, these appeared under a variety of nom-de-plumes, including Armand Rodriguez, Reggie Astor, Karl Brisse and even Luigi Mordelli.

Each year saw the birth of another super cinema, with ever more wonderful architectural attractions and innovations. The Hyams Brothers, who had built the Trocadero where my friend Van Dam played, had recently completed a new cinema called The Troxy, in the East End's Commercial Road. It seated about 4,000 people, and had a magnificent stage with one huge revolving stage in the centre and two smaller revolves on either side. The organ was a three-manual Wurlitzer and was played by Bobby Pagan, with whom I later worked a good deal.

When Joe Muscant's contract ended at the Commodore he was appointed Musical Director at the Troxy, and took most of his

44

With my parents and brother Jack.

The Mordish-Greenbaum Piano Trio.

The struggling composer meets another deadline.

At the Wurlitzer, the Gaumont State, Kilburn.

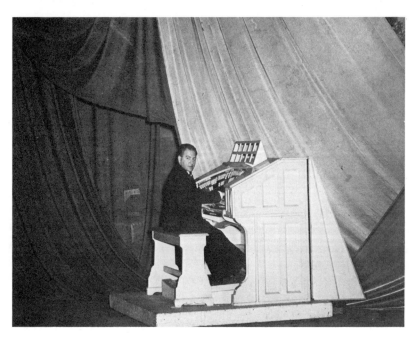

On stage at the Astoria, Old Kent Road.

orchestra with him. Financial limitations forced him to reduce the orchestra by one musician. He decided to cut out the bass-player, which meant that my left-hand had to be doubly strong. We still continued to broadcast, though without the magic name of the Commodore, the name of which had been taken over by Harry Davidson.

The Hyams Brothers believed in providing full value for money and invariably put on first-class stage shows with interesting new artistes such as the young American harmonica player, Larry Adler. He used the microphone to enhance his playing in a way that was revolutionary, and I still recall his fantastic performances of *Smoke gets in your eyes* and Ravel's *Bolero*.

Another famous American artiste who appeared at the Troxy was Belle Baker, a comedienne who also sang in the style of Sophie Tucker. During her week there she got to like my style of accompanying. She asked me whether I would care to go as her accompanist the following week to the Shakespeare Theatre, Liverpool. I was flattered. And when Joe gave me leave, I realized this would be another new experience, as this time I would be on stage as an artiste's personal accompanist rather than being a mere musician in the orchestra pit. Belle stayed at the Adelphi Hotel, Liverpool, as befitted a star. I stayed in digs in Lime Street – an eye-opener for me. My first breakfast included lumps of over-cooked fried egg swimming in fat. Across the table three dancers were engaged in a continuous quarrel. Such was the world of show business!

Some weeks later, Belle Baker phoned to say that she'd been invited to a dinner given by the Galleries-First-Nighters Club. The guest of honour was Douglas Fairbanks Junior. She would be expected to sing. Would I like to come along as her guest and accompany her on the piano? I agreed. But on the morning of this occasion disaster struck. She went down with a cold and lost her voice. Would I please go and offer her apologies? The function was held at the Criterion Restaurant in Piccadilly. All the guests, resplendent in evening dress, were assembling in the reception room, chatting and sipping cocktails or studying the table-plan pinned to an easel. Not knowing anyone I wandered around aimlessly, studied the table-plan and regarded the busily talking groups of people. Suddenly a voice said, 'You seem to be a bit lost here, so I though I'd come over and say hello. My name is Douglas Fairbanks.'

And there was the tall, young figure of the famous man standing beside me, offering his hand. I was so overwhelmed I could only babble my name. He was very kind, and chatted for a little while, obviously trying to put me at ease. As guest of honour at the dinner table, he sat next to the President of the club, Leslie Bloom, who in turn was sitting next to the famous Gertrude Lawrence. The seat to the left of Douglas was vacant, reserved for Belle Baker, and the seat next to that for her guest. I took my place there feeling conspicuous and lonely, and felt even more conspicuous when he leant across and said 'Come and move up next to me. It'll be better than sitting by yourself.' So I sat next to the famous man while the other guests cast sidelong glances, wondering who on earth I was.

That year at the Troxy was full of memorable and amusing incidents. On one occasion I received a death threat. A letter arrived addressed 'to the pianist in Joseph Muscant's orchestra' – 'If you play one more of Joseph Muscant's pot-pourris or medleys you will be stricken with chest trouble and pass away within one hundred days.' It was signed 'A Petulengro Prediction'. At that period there was a man called Gypsy Petulengro who forecast the future in a popular Sunday newspaper. I showed the letter to Joe, saying 'You see, working for you is going to cost me my life.' Mystified, we phoned the editor of the newspaper, who said 'You don't have to take any notice of what he predicts, no one ever does.' Though I never discovered the writer's identity, it was clearly someone who couldn't stand the interminable medleys in Joe's broadcasts, and who, knowing I was responsible for the link-ups, thought this prediction would put an end to them. Well, it didn't. And I still have that letter.

During the summer we also gave a number of Sunday concerts at seaside resorts. On one occasion the weather was so hot that few people came to the afternoon performance. Hearing of the poor attendance, Joe said to me urgently back-stage, 'Go out and get lost. Don't ask questions, just get lost.' I wandered out along the promenade while Joe went on to the stage to declare the concert cancelled as the pianist, who was a very essential member of the orchestra, had failed to appear.

This was also the year I went abroad for the first time – to Paris. In those pre-war days, holidays abroad were virtually unknown to the public. Most people went for their annual fortnight to the long-established English resorts. People stayed at a boarding house or small private hotel and were quite happy to spend all day walking along the promenade, sitting on the sand, and listening to one of the many concert parties and pierrot shows. So going abroad for me was a great adventure. I went with one of the violinists in the orchestra, Sidney Hoddes, who had a cousin in Paris whom he'd never met. I also had an address given me by an acquaintance whose sister had married a Frenchman. We went by train to Dover, then on the boat to Calais and again on the train to Paris. I felt as bold as Christopher Columbus.

Sidney and his cousin were Polish. She was a very pretty girl, but spoke Yiddish, not English. Sidney could not speak Yiddish. So throughout our meetings I acted as interpreter – a fascinating experience. I vividly recall their beautiful, elegant apartment and genuine friendliness. It was only after the war that I learnt from Sidney how her husband was shot by the Nazis for being a Jewish intellectual.

When the engagement at the Troxy Cinema ended and Joseph Muscant had no further employment for his orchestra, I was lucky to get the job as pianist in another cinema orchestra with a man named Philip Martell. Lucky that is, because there was still a great scarcity of work in the profession. The playing we did was of a very similar nature to previous work, accompanying variety acts and presenting our own stage shows. But now we had to divide our playing time into five sessions daily – three shows at one cinema and two at another. This meant that as soon as we finished one performance at the first cinema, we had to board a specially hired coach and go straight to the next one, backwards and forwards all day. The artistes too had to give five performances daily, and they travelled with us. This had become the standard practice in the world of cine-variety as it was called, and although there were grumbles, there was little one could do about it as employment for musicians was becoming more and more difficult to find. The great economic recession was still with us, and with mass unemployment in the country, those of use who were working were glad to be in a job.

'Stately' theme and variations

One day early in 1937 my friend Van Dam, who was still Musical Director at the Trocadero, told me that one of the organists on the Hyams Brothers circuit would be leaving shortly and that I ought to have some sense and apply for the job. Although I knew virtually nothing about the cinema organ, I was really very depressed in my work. I realized that here was an opportunity to make a break.

The Hyams Brothers knew me as a pianist both in the Commodore Orchestra and in the Troxy Cinema Orchestra, both with Joseph Muscant, and because of the arrangements I had made for Van Dam, who'd spoken highly of me. The vacancy was at the Trocette in Tower Bridge Road, Bermondsey, and they allowed me to practise on the instrument. I worked hard, trying to get my feet to operate in conjunction with my hands, and learning to re-allocate the functions of my hands and legs. Let no one imagine that playing the organ is anything like playing the piano! They are two different instruments with their own technique, the only similarity being that they both have keyboards with black and white keys. Touch, the simultaneous use of different manuals, the use of the pedals, the art of registration and learning about the different types of sounds produced by wind through different types of pipes, pre-setting the sound of the desired next combination and coping with thumb pistons: these were all to be learnt, quite apart from playing the right notes.

I was auditioned by Mick Hyams the Theatre Controller, Van Dam and Bobby Pagan. I played a couple of popular songs, the 'Indian Love Call' from *Rose Marie* and a march. Mick asked me to come to his office the following morning to talk things over. He was a blunt man. When I arrived the next day he said 'You're starting at the Trocette in a fortnight, doubling between there and the Regal, Norwood. Five shows a day, and I know you've got a car so you'll provide your own transport. We'll give you a month's trial and your salary will be £10 a week.' Once again I was over the moon. For the first time in my professional career I would be on my own.

Being an organist meant a completely new approach in the world of entertainment. There were variety acts as part of the regular programme, accompanied on the Wurlitzer, and tremendous contrasts in the types of acts, styles and musical accompaniments: vocal groups, jugglers, comedians, musical acts, acrobats and illusionists, all expecting me to sound like the Palladium Orchestra with full effects. And of course, each week there was a different musical interlude. The organist decided the subject, which had to have some bearing on the current film, or act as an advance musical entertainment for a forthcoming one. He would then have to write a script. This was interesting reading matter, projected to the audience written on coated glass slides prepared by Morgans, a firm specializing in this type of work. The script had to be very carefully thought out so that the audience would not spend all its time reading. They were expected to listen too! Again, the slides should not contain just a few words to be stared at, and they had to be faded in or out very carefully so as to make the interlude a musical one instead of a literary occasion. A good operator was an invaluable help to an organist.

There could be anything from twenty to forty slides per interlude, and I would make notes on my music to enable me to press the switch fixed to the side of the manual at the right place so that the buzzer in the operating box would warn the operator to change the slide. All this in addition to reading the music, watching the screen to see that the correct slides were being shown and playing.

Musical subjects in those days before TV covered an enormous range, and organists provided interesting musical interludes encompassing all fields of public interest. Subjects varied from 'Top Tunes of the Moment', 'An Evening in Vienna', 'In the Days of the Music Hall', 'Gilbert and Sullivan Favourites', 'Irving Berlin Favourites' to highbrow selections such as 'Music from the Ballet'.

I shall never forget my first day as a solo organist. Having rehearsed the interludes on the Monday morning with the projectionists, I was ready for the worst. The early shows at each cinema were comparatively smooth; few people were in the audience at that time of day and although I was a bit nervous, all went well. The real test was the final performance on the Monday evening. It was a working-class area where there was no other form of entertainment readily available; all the youngsters used to come in to the Trocette for the last house. They were ready, willing and able to show their pleasure or distaste for any form of entertainment. Films or performers were equal targets!

So it was with a feeling of dread that I saw the screen announce 'Louis Mordish at the Organ'. I pressed the button. The organ rose up on its lift and I presented my first interlude for approval or rebuke. I began with a selection of popular songs (I'd been advised to play these as my breaking-in performance). The words on the screen encouraged the audience to sing along. Throughout this selection, I was aware of a hubbub of voices and other noises behind me. Caught in the unwavering spotlight, I feared the worst. 'This is it,' I thought, 'they're chi-iking me – they're giving me the bird.'

Perspiration poured down my forehead. Seated in the midst of the noises, I felt I wanted to press the 'down' button, jump off the organ seat and escape. Yet I completed the interlude, finally bringing the organ down with the sea of noises still behind me. Worried, I made my way backstage to the manager's office, preparing a speech of resignation. When I saw him he was beaming, and before I could say a word said, 'Louis, that was great, very very good, keep it up old chap, keep it up.'

'But what about all that terrible noise in the audience?' I asked.

'Oh, that's their way of showing they liked what you were doing. They loved it.'

And so I was accepted. During my second week, all the organists were summoned to a special meeting in Mick Hyam's office to discuss what plans they had made for a special super interlude to commemorate the coronation of George VI. Still being very much the new boy, I was almost overawed at being at the same meeting with Quentin Maclean, Sidney Torch, Bobby Pagan and one or two others. Each of them explained his ideas to Mick. When he asked me what ideas I had, I said, 'Well, I haven't thought about it at all as I'm only here on a month's trial.'

'Oh,' he said, 'don't worry about that, you're one of us now.'

'In that case,' I said, 'with Mr Maclean's permission, I would like to do the same interlude as he will be doing.' I looked at him with some trepidation. After all, he was the country's leading cinema organist

51

and acknowledged by every other organist as such, and here was I, the new boy, daring to borrow his ideas.

'Oh sure,' he said 'you go ahead, its OK with me.' And thus it was that I joined the ranks of the Hyams Brothers organists.

During my years as organist many amusing incidents occurred, most of them unintentional. Probably the most memorable of them, if memorable may be considered the right word, happened when I went to the Gaumont State Cinema in Kilburn in response to an urgent phone call from Van Dam. The cinema was the latest of the Hyams Brothers chain and was probably the most magnificent cinema in Europe. It seated about four thousand and was a super-luxury theatre, with Van Dam as its Musical Director and Sidney Torch as the organist with a mighty four-manual Wurlitzer to play. The particular stage presentation that week featured Van Dam's orchestra and Sidney at the organ. He had just had an accident to his foot which prevented him from playing. Without the organ, the interlude could not take place, so I hurried to the State to take over as the first stage show at 2.30 pm. I moved as quickly as I could, but by the time I reached the cinema, the film programme had already started.

With an hour to spare, Van took me to Lyons for a cup of tea, in order to explain the music. 'We start here,' he said, pointing to a place on one copy. 'Play down to here, cut over to here, you pick up and then make a modulation to the next key of the following piece, we all join in and play from here to here, then it's your solo after which you modulate into the next piece.'

My mind began to boggle. The interlude, which included quite a number of organ solos, covered a wide range of music and was due to last about twenty minutes. No two organs are alike – I had never seen this particular organ – nor indeed taken part in any presentation at the State Cinema. I had to get over to the organ to have a quick look before the show. We went over to the cinema and found the duty electrician, who showed me the way under the stage to the orchestra pit. Opening the heavy metal doors, he shone his torch over the organ console, which was in complete darkness under a moveable overhead flap.

I had heard that this particular instrument was specially designed by Quentin Maclean for the State cinema. It had a most unusual layout. Name-tabs of different ranks (tone-colours), which are normally in groups, were set out in long straight lines so that it was extremely difficult to locate any particular tab at a glance; the arrangement really needed knowing. Added to that the organ seat was, to me, very strangely designed, consisting of two long padded cushions shaped to take the underneath of the thighs, their rear ends fastened together with the front opening out on a spring and the whole fastened to a fixed metal support. When I sat on it, still in the dark, my feet were about four inches above the pedal notes.

There were numerous buttons on either side of the lowest manual – five to the right and six to the left, all of which were white. They operated as follows: on the right, first button to start the organ motor, second to stop it, third to open the sliding flap over the organ, fourth to stop it anywhere and fifth to close it. On the left: first button to start operating the organ lift and bring the organ up to stage level, second to stop it anywhere, third to take it down again, fourth to turn the whole organ round, fifth to stop it anywhere and sixth to turn it back again. When the organ rose from the pit, it did so with its back to the audience and the player could not be seen until he caused it to revolve clockwise.

By this time the film had ended. I heard the main tabs closing and then the voice of Van Dam announcing over the sound system that owing to the indisposition of Sidney Torch, there would be a young deputy-organist who had only just arrived. He was sure the audience would appreciate the fact that the newcomer would do his best in these difficult circumstances. The orchestra started playing, I joined in and then, pressing the various white buttons, opened the flap, brought the organ up and round, stopped it at the right place where I could see the orchestra on the stage, and bravely tackled the music stacked on the music-stand. This was the highest stand I've ever come across. To turn the music, I had to extend my right arm upwards while leaning forward to gain additional inches. I was precariously perched on the organ stool, my feet barely touching the pedals. Then, when I actually started playing, the very first time I ever put my hands on the keys, I discovered there was a time-lag because of the distance between the organ console and the organ chambers on the opposite side of the theatre. There was a split second between the playing and the hearing of the notes – something calculated to throw any unfamiliar performer off his musical balance.

However, with one eye on the music, one eye on the conductor, one eye on the organ, one eye on the musical cuts, one eye on the name tabs, and feet trying to make normal contact with the pedals, I battled on. The show went quite well. The organ was brought down and the flap closed above my head. I made my way past the heavy metal doors, which had been opened by an attendant, on to the stage to be greeted by a smiling Van Dam. 'Well,' he said, 'everything went off fine. You can relax now. You've done it once and it'll be the same for the rest of the week.'

I was less nervous before the second performance. After all, I had already played for one show and now knew more or less what to expect. I pressed various buttons to open the flap and operate the organ lift. To my horror nothing happened! I panicked, frantically pressing the white buttons which I could see out of the corner of my eye, while trying to read the music and play at the same time. I became aware that the organ was rising, was turning, was going down, was rising, was turning. And suddenly it was dark! I had taken the organ down again, while the spotlight was shining above me on the place where I should have been.

The audience was laughing. I felt awful. I had a good look at the buttons, none of which carried any sort of name or direction. Bracing myself, I pressed buttons in turn until I knew I had brought the organ up again. I was playing and reading the music at the same time. I felt myself enveloped by the spotlight into which I had risen, could hear the roars of laughter from the audience. Grimly, I kept on playing, realizing they were thinking it was all a very carefully planned stunt to gain their sympathy.

Afterwards, I went backstage to apologize to everyone for the disaster. But they were laughing as well. The stage manager said to me, 'I forgot to tell you we have a duplicate set of controls on the stage, and for the first show you didn't actually operate them, because we knew you had quite enough to cope with and worry about without having to think about controls.' I heard later that the head of the firm, Phil Hyams, had been watching the show from the circle and had been doubled-up with laughter at my antics. He later sent a request to me asking whether I would care to do the same thing each performance. Though I felt he didn't really mean it, I declined the request all the same.

Thus it was for some time: I played my regular interludes at my own cinema and occasionally appeared as 'guest organist' at other cinemas on the circuit and frequently joined Sidney Torch and Phil

Park at the Regal Cinema, Edmonton, in a six-handed presentation. The Regal had a really magnificent stage with revolves, and some of our presentations were outstanding. We all played grand pianos and the three of them were placed in a straight line at a slight angle to the audience so that the keyboards were visible. We three pianists had our backs to each other; that is, the pianist on the extreme left was looking at the back of the centre pianist who in turn looked at the back of the player on the extreme right. Each piano had a long mirror fixed to the inside lid of the keyboard with a long strip-light at the top of each mirror. For the start of the show, the stage was completely blacked out but the strip-lights were switched on. As soon as we started playing the curtains opened, and all that the audience could see were three pairs of hands moving up and down the keyboards and reflected in the lit mirrors. A striking sight. We got on very well together and began to record for Columbia records under the name of *The Six Keyboards* – being the three keyboards of the organ played by Sidney and the three of the pianos.

In between those engagements, I worked on another composition. Like everyone else, I was fascinated by America, and by the varying atmosphere of that country as shown on the screen, particularly the bustle and excitement of New York. So much so that I wrote an orchestral suite entitled *New York*, the three movements being 'Rush Hour', 'Skyline' and 'The Great White Way'. It was an attempt to bridge the gap between so called straight and dance music, and was scored for a full normal orchestra plus a conventional dance band with saxophones, full brass and modern rhythm sections. In those days it was unheard of for large orchestras to play dance-rhythm types of music; the two worlds of straight and dance music were kept strictly apart.

New York was accepted for publication by the firm of Jacques Liber, a shrewd, likeable man who specialized in the continental type of piece, and who had already published one of my early paso dobles. It had many radio performances and practically every BBC house orchestra played it. A section was even used as a ballet by Harold Turner, a very famous dancer. I never saw the ballet as it was performed in the early days of the war; because of the difficulties of travelling through the black-out, I arrived too late at the theatre to see it. One London evening newspaper, *The Star*, printed an article saying 'To-night, Harold Turner gives the first performance of a ballet set to the music of 'Rush Hour' from *New York* Suite written by the American composer Louis Mordish.' The particular writer of the article was taken aback when I phoned to tell him that I was not American and that the nearest I had ever been to that country was Llandudno.

March militaire

Meanwhile, the European situation was steadily deteriorating. With the invasion of Danzig in Poland by Hitler on 1st September, the frantic comings and goings of British and French diplomats came to nothing and war was declared in the memorable radio speech by Neville Chamberlain two days later. None of us who were listeners will ever forget the emotions and feelings at that awful moment. Fifteen minutes after the broadcast, when the very first air-raid warning sirens began to wail, everyone expected Hitler's Luftwaffe to appear and destroy London as they had destroyed Rotterdam weeks before.

With the declaration of war everything changed. A full blackout at night was immediately introduced. Cars had their lights covered by shields with small crosses cut out to permit a very small amount of light to be seen. There were no lighted shop windows and all households were heavily covered with blackout material or brown paper, and pedestrians made their way at night with the aid of small torches. There were the ever watchful eyes of the Civil Defence and air-raid wardens who were always quick to shout 'Put that light out' if a householder inadvertently lit his room before fixing his blackout. It was a period of hesitancy and uncertainty. Food and petrol were rationed. Many articles were immediately in very short supply. All entertainments closed down including cinemas and theatres. Many smaller businesses ceased trading and everyone just waited to see what would happen. Was their particular job important? Was it going to last. How long before the Germans began to invade?

When they didn't, things began to get back to a sort of restricted normality. It was the period that came to be known as the 'phoney war'. Cinemas and theatres re-opened, though on a restricted scale. My own job was restored but under different conditions. I was transferred to the Gaumont Cinema at Watford, still with the Hyams

Brothers, where for a brief period I combined the duties of organist with that of assistant manager. Not that I knew much about managing a cinema, but with the calling up of so many men into the Forces, everyone had to do something else.

By law all men were required to register for military service. I wanted to join the RAF. I could drive, and thought I might make a useful transport driver. But at the end of my examination, having thanked me for my offer, the medical officer said, 'We cannot accept you because you wear glasses, and if a shell or bomb exploded near you, your glasses would break and you would then become a liability to us instead of an asset. You'll be called up for the Army in due course. Good morning.'

And so I returned to the cinema, now also my home. In June 1939 I'd married Gwen Cibolia, a young girl I'd met at a Christmas party the previous year. Knowing that it would not be long before I had to join the Forces, I'd put our furniture in store, and my wife joined me in the cinema. We lived in one of the dressing-rooms, the idea being that when I did have to go, she would stay with her parents. Naturally, we all hoped the war would not last long so that we would be able to set up house again somewhere with our own furniture.

The manager of the cinema was Denis Norden – a very young manager indeed. With men everywhere being called-up, including of course the regular managers of the circuit, some going into Civil Defence or the Fire Brigade and others going into the Forces, young Denis took over when there was a shortage of more experienced men. But he was very able. We worked well together, he as manager and I as his assistant. Frequently, after the cinema had closed at night, we would share a little late-night musical session at the Wurlitzer (he also lived in a dressing-room) and one of the songs which will always be with me is Jerome Kern's *All the things you are*, which I first played in the small hours between an 'all clear' and another air-raid warning siren. I still think it one of the greatest songs of its kind ever written: a haunting melody with beautiful harmonic changes and so much development in just thirty-two bars.

One day, Denis and I were talking about the war and how it was influencing young people's lives and careers. He was very depressed and said, 'Should something happen to me when I go into the Forces, I'll have achieved nothing. No-one will know that I ever lived; there'll be nothing to remember me by. Whereas if the worst should happen

58

to you, at least your name will still be in print on your musical compositions. Someone somewhere will be able to recall your name.' He needn't have worried; his name is certainly well-known today!

Time slowly drifted by. My wife, an expectant mother, was evacuated to a safe part of the country and in due course my daughter Arlene was born in Hayle, Cornwall. After some weeks they both returned to our dressing-room in the cinema. I realized of course that I was just filling in time until my call-up papers would arrive for me to enter the Army. Not a happy prospect.

At that time, the RAF had its regular Central Band, and knowing that entertainment was a psychological necessity in war-time, was forming a number of five-piece units to send to its camps far and wide. The reasoning was that it was much more sensible to have entertainment supplied by professionals. After all, it was easier to train a musician in such duties as a store-keeper or pay-clerk rather than to make a storeman into a musician and entertainer.

One day Van Dam rang to say he'd suggested to the RAF the idea of forming an orchestra of about twenty-five musicians, with the function of providing all kinds of music for RAF personnel wherever they were stationed. The proposed orchestra would not be another dance band or a military band, but something to cater for middlebrow tastes. The RAF were impressed, and gave Van the go-ahead. He would be given the rank of Warrant Officer as soon as the orchestra was complete. The men would join the RAF as musicians for their official duties. I jumped at his offer that I should join the orchestra as pianist. I had to enter the Services anyway, and I would be happiest to do so playing music. But there was a catch if I wanted to be his pianist: I would have to volunteer for the RAF straight away; I had to be in the RAF before my Army call-up papers arrived. I discussed the matter with my wife. We agreed that it made sense. I told Van, and he called for me in his car the following day so that we could drive to the RAF musical headquarters at Uxbridge to discuss the matter with G. P. O'Donnell, the head of the central band.

Van had his interview. He came out smiling. O'Donnell had been on to the Air Ministry, and they'd arranged for me to come in straight away. I couldn't believe it. Surely I wasn't all that important. I went back to the Watford Cinema where I was told the Air Ministry had phoned while I was out, and would I please phone the number given me straight away. Dazed, I did so. I spoke to the Wing-Commander:

'We understand that you're a very important man in this new orchestra idea. We'd like to have you in with us straight away. We've made arrangements with our Edgware recruiting office for you to be picked up outside your cinema tomorrow morning at eight. You'll be brought to the recruiting office for a formal medical examination, then you'll go over to Uxbridge where you'll be sworn into the RAF.'

The next morning at the recruiting office, a misty cold morning in January, I was led through a series of rooms where I got the impression that all the staff were waiting just for me. 'Sign here please Mr Mordish. This way Mr Mordish. Sign this form Mr Mordish. Follow me Mr Mordish', until I reached the medical examination room. I was quickly given a going over and passed as A3, which meant that I was physically fit apart from the fact that I wore glasses. 'Take these travel vouchers Mr Mordish – make you way to Uxbridge and you'll be sworn in straight away.'

I was dazed by the time I got to East Camp, Uxbridge. I was told to enter the little house where all new recruits reported, and after my particulars had been noted by a clerk, to wait until I was called to the swearing-in room. By now it was about 11.30 am. I waited patiently in the upstairs waiting-room, sitting with other young men on long wooden forms. At 1 pm someone announced they were closing for lunch for an hour and told us to go to the NAAFI, get a meal and report back. With several other recruits, I made my way there and had my first experience of Service food. As a civilian I had to pay. The less said about the experience the better.

I reported back at 2 pm, went upstairs again and sat on the same form waiting for my name to be called. Men were arriving all the time. They waited a while, their names were called, they went downstairs, were sworn in and disappeared, while new recruits who had been arriving and waiting repeated the process. This went on until 5 pm. All this time I had been sitting patiently. At last a corporal came upstairs to say they'd finished for the day. Those of us who had not yet been sworn in should report back at 9 o'clock the next day. When I returned to the cinema, I was greeted with astonishment. I had taken my farewell leave as a hero to do his bit for King and Country. And here I was back again. I carefully explained what had happened and later in the day said 'goodbye' again to everybody.

Next morning I was back in Uxbridge at the appointed time. Once again I waited very patiently until 1 pm, was told to go and have

Our five-piece band entertains the troops.

Soloist with the RAF Technical Training Command Orchestra.

Louis Mordish, conductor.

At the Gaumont State Wurlitzer again, some years later . . .
(Photo: John D. Sharp)

Dickie and I meet Princess Anne, introduced by Harry Secombe.

At the Wurlitzer, Worthing Assembly Hall.
(Photo: John D. Sharp)

Worthing again, with George Blackmore, Nigel Ogden, Ena Baga and Bobby Pagan.
(Photo: John D. Sharp)

lunch, reported back and waited until 5 pm when the ritual of 'We're finished for the day' was repeated. I just could not believe it. Hundreds of young men had come upstairs, had their names called and gone downstairs where they had all been sworn in, in groups of about twenty at a time. I was still sitting waiting, stuck to my form. When I got home again that evening, nobody would believe me. I was accused of being a 'crafty one' and 'pulling a fast one', inventing the whole story and probably never even going to Uxbridge.

Back again at the camp the following morning, I waited and waited. Eventually, having seen what looked like an endless stream of men going downstairs, I decided to find out what was happening. I went downstairs, and asked why I had not been called, although I had been waiting over two days. The officer told me I was a 'nationality case'. Enquiries had been going on about the background of my Russian parents to see whether they'd been involved in any sort of political activities. I didn't know whether to be annoyed or to laugh. The idea of my parents – a couple of ordinary *Heimishe* Jews who'd years ago come to England to escape from the Russian pogroms – being vetted was ridiculous. 'However,' the officer continued, 'we think everything's in order now and we'll soon be calling you down for swearing-in.' Of course, everything was in order. After lunch, I once again took my place on the form and waited patiently. Eventually my name was called. I went downstairs and joined a group of other young men. I was the last person in the last group to be sworn in that afternoon; I was now a member of the Royal Air Force. I waited to hear my first official instructions. We were told that as the camp was full, we'd be issued with a 'sleeping-out' pass to enable us to return home, and report back at nine the next morning. Once again, I just couldn't believe it, three days since I first went to Uxbridge to join the ranks and here I was, going home yet again.

We spent the next few days at camp getting kitted out with equipment and doing nothing except talking to other musicians who were all waiting to be fitted into small five-piece units and then sent to a base for duties. I went home each evening, just like office hours. During those early days I received no training of any kind and didn't even know who I was supposed to salute, not yet knowing the difference between an NCO and a commissioned officer. I found the safest way was always to follow another airman and if he saluted someone then I did the same. However, this strategy was not always foolproof. Before I was posted, the station Warrant Officer sent for me. I quickly went to his office. I tapped at his door and when a voice said 'come in' I entered and, not knowing the rules, took off my hat. 'Put your bloody hat on,' he roared, 'you're improperly dressed.' The next day, I had to help carry some crates of drink into the Officers' Mess and remembering the Warrant Officer shouting at me, kept my hat on while actually entering the Mess. Several voices shouted at me 'Take your bloody hat off when you enter the Officers' Mess.'

After about two or three weeks of idling about (several of us were actually waiting for the complete intake of Van Dam's orchestra), I was posted officially on temporary duty to an RAF camp at Newton in Nottingham, where the pianist had fallen ill. I arrived there, complete with service kitbag, and was met at the station by an RAF van which took me back to camp. There was hardly any time to unpack, for the band was due to play at an Officers' Mess dance. I finished my first Service engagement at about 2.30 am; by the time I got into my bed in the cold Nissen hut, it was almost 3 am. I moved around by torchlight as many men were asleep. Then, at 6.30 am the light suddenly snapped on, there was a terrific banging of fists on the metal walls of the lockers and shouts of 'Come on you lot – everybody out for PT.' My bed was nearest the door. Suddenly, somebody threw my blankets off and shouted 'Come on there – get up then.' Not knowing that I could have pleaded that I had been on late duty, not having received any instructions of any kind as to my rights (which allowed me to stay in bed), I staggered up and joined the others for exercise outside the Nissen huts on a parade ground. It had been snowing during the night and was freezing.

I went for breakfast feeling very cold and terribly tired. Later that morning I told one of the other musicians who shared the hut that I didn't feel well, and wanted to see the camp doctor. He replied that I could only see the doctor on the morning sick parade.

'But I feel bad,' I replied, 'I can't wait until tomorrow morning.'

'Then you must get a special chit from your NCO,' he said.

'What's a chit and who is my NCO?' I asked. One of the other men in the hut told me that the Duty Officer might give me a chit to see the doctor. Someone gave me directions. The Duty Officer was extremely annoyed that I had come to him, and rebuked me for not reporting sick at the proper time or getting my NCO to give me a chit. But he did give me written authority to see the camp doctor immediately, who diagnosed acute pharyngitis, and immediately arranged for an ambulance to take me to Nottingham hospital, where I was put in the same ward as the pianist I'd come up to replace. I wrote home saying where I was. When my mother heard I was in hospital, she was convinced that I had been wounded in military action.

On my return to Uxbridge I learnt that Van Dam had been rejected at his RAF medical because he was in such poor physical condition. A very heavy smoker, he wore glasses with exceptionally thick lenses and suffered from stomach ailments. He could not even be accepted as a Grade C3 musician. So his whole theatre orchestra scheme collapsed. I and several other musicians who had hoped to be in that unit were left without the special posting for which we had volunteered. We were now individuals to be fitted into any five-piece unit which might need our services.

About a week or so later, I was called into the room dealing with postings and asked if I would like to be a member of a five-piece unit being formed under the leadership of a violinist named Jack Mandel. He and the other three proposed members were also in the room: Albert Aldcroft, the accordionist; Alfred Ralston, clarinet and sax player; and Sid Wright, the drummer. I had never worked with any of them before, and apart from having seen them in the large general room where all of us in the central band department congregated, did not know them. We were all about the same age. As I had no option, I agreed.

And so another five-piece unit came into being. We were posted to Coltishall in Norfolk, an airfield in Fighter Command. Upon arrival we reported to the Station Warrant Officer, who told us what our station duties would be; as far as actual playing duties were concerned, we were under the control of the Entertainments Officer. We soon settled down to our new duties: in the mornings, the care of the very large NAAFI hall where all social functions took place, duties such as swilling out the tiled floor, arranging the chairs and tables for a station show or concert, or re-arranging them so that the hall was suitable for dances and other functions. The large camp had, in addition to the pilots, engineers and technicians, a large complement of WAAFS, who worked in occupations ranging from clerks to intelligence officers. Our little band played for camp dances, Officers' Mess functions, NCO dances and camp shows. Part of each day was spent rehearsing and arranging a repertoire of music suitable for any occasion; coupled with our NAAFI swilling duties, it was a full-time job. We were an excellent quintet, not just a dance band, and able to cover a wide range of music. We became popular both with the officers and the 'erks', or ordinary ranks, and our music was always well received.

I recall the occasion when Sir Arthur Barrett, the CO of the station, attended the Officers' Mess dances. He was about sixty; and as we very soon found out from his frequent requests sent up to us by his junior officers, very fond of Viennese waltzes. But instead of dancing three steps to a bar, he danced one, which meant that he was moving rather slowly. He was always sending up requests for us to play faster; but whenever he partnered a pretty young WAAF officer, he liked the dance to last as long as possible, forcing us to continue with waltz after waltz. The rest of the officers and their ladies, trying to get their three steps into each bar, were moving frantically, becoming hot and bothered in their full uniform, and glaring at us as they passed the bandstand. But nobody dared stop dancing, not while the CO was still on the floor. They could have killed us, but we just kept on playing fast 'oom-pah-pah' music and watching the CO's feet until even he had had enough. And this sort of dance happened quite frequently.

I managed to find accommodation for my wife and daughter in a small council house; two up, two down in a terrace of eight, occupied by an agricultural family in Buxton Lamass. A sleeping-out pass meant that after I finished my camp duties I could leave the station and return home about three miles away. Of course, I had to report back to camp each morning, and in order to make the journey I bought an old bicycle, a ladies' model with high handlebars. The only water supply to the row of houses came from a well, about half-way along the row and about twenty yards from the back walls. I would go and get the water in a bucket when I was home, wading through the mud in wet weather and in fine weather watching that spiders were not brought up with the water. There was no indoor toilet, nor a proper one outside, just a cesspool about fifteen yards from the house.

The tenant was a young, red-faced man, stockily built like a real-life John Bull. His name was Herbert Spinks, and he paid 4s. 6d. a week rent. I well recall his anger when the local council informed him that it proposed to bring piped water from the nearest mains into the house, and to fit one tap into the little kitchen. For this service, the rent would be increased by fourpence per week. He was furious. 'What do we want tap-water for in the house. What's wrong with the well-water. We've been using it for years. What do we want these new-fangled things for!' As an agricultural worker, he was in a reserved occupation and was not eligible for military service as his work was deemed necessary for the continuation of essential services. For his labour, he received the princely sum of 17s. 6d. weekly. One day he came home from his work shouting: 'Kathy, Kathy, I got news! We're going to get a rise. We're going to get £1 a week now. That's good news isn't it, Kathy!'

I had been at Coltishall some months when I received a letter informing me that my application to join the RAF had been refused and I would have to join the Army in the Pioneer Corps. A travel warrant was enclosed with a note informing me that if I failed to report, I would be treated as a deserter and arrested. I wrote back politely saying it would appear that an error had been made somewhere as I was already in the RAF and quoted my service number.

A major event of this Coltishall period was my first broadcast as a theatre organist. It was the time of the 'phoney war' when very little military activity was taking place. I had written to the BBC saying how much I would like to be given the opportunity to broadcast on the organ, at that time an extremely popular light-music medium. However, I was still surprised when I received a letter from a Mr Anderson of the Outside Broadcasts Department offering a date. It was to be from the Ambassador Cinema in Hendon on Friday, 30th May 1941. I was to be given a full fifteen minutes at 8.30 am; I realised, of course, that this short programme was to be in the nature of an audition.

The Station Warrant Officer was thrilled that one of his lads was going to London to broadcast to the world and I obtained a special pass without any bother. The first session was quite an experience. I had to be in the cinema very early in the morning to set up the organ, arranging the piston combinations to suit my requirements and to do some rehearsing. It was after all quite some time since I had last played such an instrument. The only people present were the night-watchman, who had let me into the cinema, and two BBC engineers who set up the microphones and communicating lines with Broadcasting House where the announcer was waiting for his cues. During the rehearsal I was asked the title of my signature tune: I would be expected to play it at the beginning and end of my programme under the announcements. I thought quickly, and suggested *St Louis Blues*, fitting my name. Fortunately, I knew it from memory and so it was that it became my signature tune. After playing it under the opening announcement, the first notes I sent through the ether for the listening public was the selection of music from *The Student Prince* with its opening drum-roll and fanfare. Needless to say, I returned to camp a minor hero.

Less successful was my rifle training. During the first session of Sten gun instruction, the instructor showed us how to load and fire, then issued us with live bullets. 'Now men,' he said, 'some of these new-fangled Sten guns may not work properly. They're mass-produced and the makers haven't got time to check each one. Sometimes when you release the trigger after firing the gun might not stop, so be very careful and don't point the thing at anybody. Just point it at the sky until the magazine is empty.'

We pointed our guns skywards and were given the order to fire. It was a strange feeling, firing a lethal weapon with live bullets. On the order to cease fire, I released the trigger, but my gun didn't stop. The Sergeant-Instructor realized what had happened and shouted 'Don't turn for Christ's sake, just point the bloody thing upwards and keep still.' Those were anxious moments, and my arms trembled as the men all ran behind me!

After Coltishall, our quintet was posted to Bracknell, Andover in Hampshire, Reading (the HQ of 'Technical Training Command') and even to the Shetlands. We stayed at each camp from six months to a year, and were lucky not to be sent overseas. Our conditions were usually good, as we were a much appreciated little group of musicians, catering for all types of entertainment. With the exception of the sax player and drummer, we remained together for the whole of our stay in the RAF. Our particular ability to help Service men and women to forget their problems for a little while was very important and much appreciated. We would play their favourite tunes and were sometimes joined by a singer, usually one of the Servicemen, who liked to perform with the band. Where there was a village hall or church hall with a fairly decent piano, I joined in with the others. But

66

as often as not the pianos were unbelievably dreadful old crocks with half the notes out of action and the others out of tune. Sometimes we would travel in a lorry or van to some isolated spots where anti-aircraft guns were mounted. Their crews had very little to do between spells of duty, except stay in Nissen huts, sleeping or reading to while away the boredom. Our visits were highlights of their duty periods.

A major event during my time at Reading was the formation of a symphony orchestra from musicians throughout the country, bringing them all to our camp on temporary duty and giving public concerts in aid of the RAF Benevolent Fund. All these men had been professional musicians in pre-war days: some were classical players and others were dance-band musicians, others again were middle-of-the-road theatre and show-business musicians. The first trumpet player, Jackson, became first trumpet in the BBC Symphony Orchestra after the war. The oboist, who was a boiler-stoker in the RAF, was a member of the famous Hallé Orchestra.

Our Entertainments Officer was an amateur musician and bass-player, Squadron-Leader B. Hartley-Miller and his main job in the RAF was that of Catering Officer. He was a very pleasant man whose knowledge of music was – to be kind – extremely limited. He appointed himself as principal conductor because of his rank, but he was wise enough to appoint an assistant conductor, a man named Foster who had been chorus-master in the Sadler's Wells Opera company. For an orchestra which had only been in existence a fortnight, ours was an ambitious first programme, including the Grieg Piano Concerto in which I was to be the soloist. I had to do a lot of practice as I hadn't studied the work for years. Rehearsals were held in a large hall, the atmosphere much like that of a normal peace-time orchestral rehearsal, except that the musicians were all in uniform, and prefaced their queries with 'Sir, excuse me . . .'

I was very helpful to Hartley-Miller on a number of occasions. Once, as I was discussing a technical point with him, the trumpet player Jackson came over to us and said, 'Excuse me, did I hear your name right? Mordish? Are you related to the composer Mordish?' I told him that I was indeed one and the same. 'Well, I've played a lot of his numbers with the BBC Midland Light Orchestra. I always thought he was a middle-aged man and we all somehow assumed that to be right. Anyway, I'm glad to meet you.'

The first concert was held at Reading Town Hall on Sunday 30th April 1944. It was a great success and a momentous occasion for me because I had never before played a concerto with an orchestra in public. I think that for a performer, this must be one of the greatest musical thrills: the purely orchestral passages, then the entering of the solo part, the weaving together of soloist and orchestra, the give and take between the two. It was an extraordinary feeling, which was repeated when I was fortunate enough to do some recording sessions with the RAF Services Entertainment Unit, on one occasion playing the solo in Gershwin's *Rhapsody in Blue*, recorded in its entirety by a first-class orchestra, all pre-war professionals, conducted by Sidney Torch.

The success of the Reading concerts encouraged the officers concerned to continue with the plan. They now became ambitious, and wanted international artists as soloists, not just ordinary airmen. For their next concert, they engaged Moura Lympany to play the Tchaikovsky First Piano Concerto. But for all the orchestral rehearsals, which took place days before the concert, I played the solo part. This was also a great experience for me, because as far as I was concerned, each performance was a public concert, and I was able to perform with full symphony orchestra the Grieg and Tchaikovsky Concertos, Mozart's A major, and Beethoven's 'Emperor' and C minor Concertos.

The film *Dangerous Moonlight*, with its wartime heroics and romance had made the *Warsaw Concerto* immensely popular. It was often requested by the CO's wife, Lady Barrett, whenever our little quintet played at an Officers' Mess function. On the evening of the concert when Moura Lympany played the Tchaikovsky Concerto – magnificently I should add – she was entertained to dinner by the CO and his officers, all accompanied by their ladies. Our quintet provided soft 'dinner music' during the meal. The head table was only about ten feet from the bandstand, with the backs of the guests towards us, and the guest of honour sitting next to the CO. The other tables extended the length of the room from the top table towards the furthest wall from us. We played the usual type of music for such occasions: a waltz and a musical comedy selection.

During pauses, one of the quintet quietly laid a bet that Lady Barrett would send up a request for the *Warsaw Concerto*. I could not believe she would be so undiplomatic, but I was wrong. Sure enough, after a while, an officer came up to the stand and told our corporal that Lady Barrett would like us to play the very piece.

I was dumbfounded. This was not a request. This was an order. And from the CO's wife. How could she be so tactless as to ask for a 'pseudo concerto' when that very afternoon she had heard such a brilliant performance by the guest of honour. But that was not all. Several young officers came on to the little bandstand, and with much ado, pulled my grand piano to the very front of the stand and opened the lid with a great show of enthusiasm. There was I, in front, playing our arrangement, while all the guests stopped eating, and copying the example of Lady Barrett, turned in their seats so that they could all give their full attention to the performance.

I have never forgotten my embarrassment, both at the fact that I was being expected to play what could only be described as a piece of light popular music in what had suddenly become a concert hall, and that Moura Lympany had been placed in such an awkward situation, being compelled to listen because everybody else was doing so. During the piece I kept wondering how she would react. I was overwhelmed when, during the applause which followed (there had to be applause because the CO and his wife were both clapping enthusiastically), she got up from her chair, walked to the bandstand, and congratulated me on my very fine performance. A diplomatic lady.

There was one concert which did not have a soloist, and the officers who arranged it thought it might be a novel idea to have one of my compositions included in the programme, along with one by a visiting officer-conductor. I was delighted to be given this opportunity of a performance, and I must say that my particular officer was always kind and helpful to me at all times. However, I was not so pleased when I realized that my piece would only be run through a couple of times with the orchestra, while the visiting officer-conductor went over and over his piece!

One of the works played at this concert was William Walton's 'Spitfire' Prelude and Fugue. For this I joined the percussion section of the orchestra. I was the cymbals player, and had nothing during the whole piece until almost the very end when I had to hit them hard. The particular part I was reading had no instrumental cues to help follow the piece, just 'bars rest'. So I counted the bars, and counted and counted, and continued to count frantically as I realized the conductor was just beating time and not giving any cues to the players. 'Where the hell are we now?' one of my colleagues muttered.

'Watch me,' I muttered back. 'When I hit the cymbals, you hit the drum.'

We were both panicking as the piece got more and more exciting. I hit the cymbals together with an almighty clang. And by a miracle I was right!

On another occasion, I was the percussionist in a military band. At one of the camps to which we'd been posted, there was an amateur station band which was mainly a brass band. The sergeant decided to make use of our talents, and obtained permission for us to join his band on ceremonial occasions. As I could not play a brass instrument, he decided to make me the bass drum player (I 'knew how to keep the tempo right in the marches'). Accordingly, on the first parade, two big hefty airmen were placed alongside of me, one on either side, to help hook the drum on to the special support which had been put round my neck for this purpose. When the order was given, they duly raised the drum from the ground and hooked it in position. The band began to play and we all marched forward with me banging the drum. But with the bass drum resting on my chest, I could barely see over the top of it and the men on either side had to steer me gently when it became necessary. When we reached the end of a particular tune and the musicians could put their instruments down, I was unable to unhook the drum. The men on either side tried to help but as we were all still marching, it was impossible. I adopted the easy method, stopped marching, and wrestling with the hook with the assistance of the two men, finally easing it off the support. In the meantime, all the men behind me continued to march forward. I was not asked to play the bass drum again on marches or parades.

Because of the very favourable opinion of me held by our entertainments officer, I was sometimes able to get a day's pass to travel from Reading to London to give an organ broadcast. On one occasion I was due to be on the air at about 10 am from the Empire Cinema, Leicester Square. I decided to arrive at the theatre the previous night, in order to catch a few hours sleep and some rehearsal-time before the broadcast.

I arrived at the Empire Cinema about 2 am. The blackout was in full force, and I made my way there knowing that the building would be locked. I hoped to find a night watchman. But I couldn't find an entrance of any kind. I tried shaking the iron gates. They were locked. Realizing there was not a way of getting through, I decided to climb over to try one of the front doors. I began clambering up in the darkness. Then, as in all good story books, I suddenly felt a hand on my leg. I looked down as saw a policeman shining a torch in my face. He remained convinced I was a drunken serviceman until I showed him the music in my satchel.

In another incident, I was actually sitting at the console five minutes before the transmission was due to begin when I was given a telegram from Sandy MacPherson, the BBC staff organist in charge of all programmes. The message read: *IT IS IMPERATIVE THAT THERE ARE NO BREAKS WHATSOEVER BETWEEN ITEMS. IMPROVISE MODULATIONS SO THAT THERE ARE NO GAPS IN ORDER TO MINIMIZE THE POSSIBILITY OF ENEMY PROPAGANDA BEING INSERTED IN ANY WAY.*

One of the more memorable moments during my five years in uniform was a meeting with Eric Partridge, the famous lexicographer and literary authority. It happened at Andover camp. Several of us were sitting off-duty in the NAAFI. My eyes caught sight of a notice on the wall which proclaimed *NO SMOKING ALLOWED*. Feeling the need for some scintillating discussion, I pointed out that the notice was wrong. You can't allow something that doesn't exist to take place, and 'No Smoking' is something that doesn't exist. It should have said *SMOKING IS NOT ALLOWED*.

This all led to a heated argument, which was resolved when someone said to me, 'Go and ask that man sitting over there in the corner. He's Eric Partridge, and he should know.'

'Who's Eric Partridge?' I asked. I was given a withering look and told that he was one of the greatest living authorities on the English language! I felt abashed, but went over to him, excused myself for interrupting his reading and stated my case.

He thought for a moment, then said, 'Tell your friends that you're right, because you cannot turn a negative into a positive.'

After that first meeting, I would try and talk to him as often as possible, glad to be able to learn from him. He was a bit of a mystery man: tall, gaunt and scholarly. He would have looked more at home in a professor's cap and gown than in his ill-fitting service uniform. We could not understand why such an intellectual man was just a clerk – not even a corporal – when many of the officers were so patently his inferiors. He looked distinctly out of place when marching with other men.

One day he told me he was going to have a little party to celebrate his fiftieth birthday. Another mystery: what was a man of his age doing clerking in the RAF? At this party, he proposed having three guests: a young Welshman of nineteen named Keith who was a PT instructor, representing 'youth and energy'; a famous portrait painter, also in the RAF, named Angus Scott, to represent 'art'; myself to represent 'music', with Eric Partridge himself to represent 'literature'. Unfortunately, that party never took place as Angus was posted to another station and I to the Shetlands. I wrote to Eric from there, and received a reply which I think is a miniature literary masterpiece. One of my valued treasures.

In early 1944 I was posted to the Shetlands, entertaining airmen involved in the hunt for U-boats. It was a memorable visit, not least as it involved my first plane journey. The quintet went by train to Leuchars, an RAF station in Fifeshire. From there we flew in a Harrow aircraft to Sumburgh, sitting on the floor of the plane because there were no seats. The windows were blacked out because on a previous flight the men had been able to look down on the ships in Scapa Flow, and one of them had written in his letter home a description of what he saw. We lived and worked in Nissen huts which had very thick ropes slung over them, tied and secured around large boulders. Violent winds blew over the islands. We would wake up during the night fearing the hut was being blown away, and could feel it rising and trying to break the ropes. Though it was an uncomfortable existence, there were consolations. On some nights we could observe the Aurora Borealis, and during my stay there I frequently saw the Midnight Sun. It never sank below the horizon, and you could read a newspaper by the light of the sun after midnight.

Though letters from home were eagerly awaited, their arrival was often delayed by several days due to the shortage of suitable planes and doubtful flying conditions. Our letters to the mainland were censored. I learnt many months later that my letters to my mother reached her weeks after I sent them. As she could read no English, I wrote to her in Yiddish, and there were no rabbis on the island to read them! They had to be sent to the mainland for reading and censoring. I often wondered what the censors thought when they

72

opened my letters and were confronted with weird looking scribble. Had I written to her in English, she would not have believed they were from me but that someone had written on my behalf as I was probably wounded and incapable of writing myself.

On 6th June 1944 news broke of the Normandy landings. After that, our activities seemed to fade into insignificance as we waited for the latest news bulletins. The change in the war situation, now that the Allies were on the offensive, created a feeling of optimism among the Service personnel. The end was in sight, and with it a return to 'Civvy Street'.

At the end of our six months in the Shetlands, we were posted back to Reading, where I remember one morning seeing the first of the 'thousand bomber raids'. The sky was full of planes of all types and sizes, flying at different heights and converging from many camps into a main stream flying towards Germany. By this time, too, I'd heard from brother Jack. He'd been in the Normandy landings, wading ashore from a landing-craft, sleeping in trenches and guarding ammunition dumps. Originally he'd been involved in Van Dam's plans for an orchestra, but his application for volunteer service had come too late. The day after posting it, he received his Army call-up papers for the Pioneer Corps, where he'd been involved in rough manual labour, not at all the sort of work for a quiet musician with delicate, violinist's hands.

We remained at Reading until the end of the war. VE Day ('Victory in Europe' Day) came on 8th May 1945, with the surrender of the Nazi forces. Everyone went as mad as the exigencies of the Service would permit. The war was not yet officially over however, as the other war in the Far East was still continuing. But after the official end of the war with the Japanese surrender, it became a case of waiting for the official demobilisation procedures to be announced.

It was some five months before I myself was actually demobbed. All personnel were put into group numbers for demobilisation purposes, effective on certain dates according to their age and length of service. As these numbers and dates were announced, so everybody in the particular group went on the appointed day to the appropriate centre to be demobbed and to re-enter civilian life. While we waited for our special day, pilots were kept occupied by giving privileged people an opportunity of seeing the devastation of the Ruhr caused by Allied bombing. Because our little band was so popular with the officers and men, we were given a special treat and taken on one of these joy-rides.

The plane seated five passengers in addition to the pilot and navigator, who were both big husky Canadians. At times the pilot forgot he had passengers because he would take the plane up to a great height, then dive at a sharp angle and bank steeply over the housetops. It was a most interesting trip. We flew very low over the French and Belgian coast line, then turned inwards to Holland. We saw some of the underwater defences meant to deter the Allies from landing their troops. Also the coastal fortifications and pill-boxes, which made us realise the enormity of the task that had confronted the Allied forces. Over the Belgian beaches, holiday-makers were enjoying the fine weather and their first free summer for years. When they waved happily at us, I couldn't help thinking that not so long ago every plane had been a menace to them. Heavy mist prevented our going on to see the ruined areas of the Ruhr. We landed at Nijmegen in Holland, and stayed for about an hour. The camp still had German notices, for only a few weeks before the area must have been swarming with German troops.

During the war my old employers, the Hyams Brothers, sold their cinema chain to Gaumont-British, one of the giant circuits in the cinema world. Realizing that when I was once more a civilian I would have to look for a job again, I decided to call on the musical supervisor of the firm on my next leave to see what my chances might be of finding employment. I duly called on him, a charming man named Harry Fryer. I was made most welcome, and was delighted to learn that I was still on the books, having been transferred to the new firm. He promised to fix me up straight away.

In due course, the great moment arrived when I would cease being a number and become an individual again. One day in October 1945 I made my way to the appointed centre where I joined a queue of men passing through the different sections of the demobbing machine, thereby acquiring a civilian suit, hat, shoes and shirt. I emerged into the world, ready to start a new life, conscious of the fact that civilian life would be vastly different from what I had known before, but ready to re-launch myself into the world of the cinema.

More variations

I left the RAF on a Tuesday. The following Monday I started an engagement at the New Victoria Cinema in London at the salary of £12 weekly, a considerable financial increase on my Service pay – about 2s. 6d. per day. The cinema was a very beautiful theatre. But whereas many cinemas on the Hyams Brothers circuit had been technically equipped to an extremely high standard with many pieces of equipment designed to help their organists' presentations – microphones, slide projectors, Brenographs (machines showing pictures on slides which could be rapidly changed or dissolved one into another and were used as backgrounds to word-slides), coloured spotlights, record-synchronisers – the New Victoria Cinema had none of these. Not even a microphone for the organist to announce the programme, until I had one installed.

At first the manager had been hostile. However, after a couple of months I completely won him over, and he would often talk to me about music. One day he said, 'You know Louis, you're too good for the sort of music you play, you ought to give them something really worthwhile. Something like *Finlandia*.' I replied that the piece was too heavy for most people who came to the cinema for light entertainment. Most of my interludes were devoted to popular light music: tunes of the moment, musical comedy songs, Gershwin, Cole Porter and others. But the manager just smiled and said, 'Next week when you change your interlude, you play *Finlandia*. And what's more, I'll announce it for you.'

Though I had misgivings, I decided to give it a go. At the conclusion of the film the following Monday, with the screen-tabs and front of stage curtains closed, the manager stepped out before the audience and in the slowest, most pompous voice imaginable announced, 'Louis Mordish will now play *Finlandia*.' It was a dreadful way to introduce an organ interlude. As he walked slowly off the stage

75

and I began playing the opening bars while bringing the organ up to stage level, I could sense that the audience was not going to like it. The audience had been antagonised even before I began playing. I resolved then and there that there would be no more managerial announcements; and no more *Finlandia*.

About this time I began broadcasting from the BBC's own organ. Although by then I had been on the air for some years, I had always broadcast from cinemas other than my own base theatre. Sandy MacPherson, the BBC staff organist responsible for booking other players, offered me a date on the BBC's own giant Möller organ, a five-manual instrument in the Jubilee Chapel in London's City Road. A small church had been converted into a broadcasting studio and the organ, previously owned by Reginald Foort, one of the earliest and most famous of cinema-organists, was housed there. (The BBC bought this Möller organ to replace the original theatre organ in the St George's Hall, next to the Queen's Hall, which had been destroyed during the war. I well remember visiting the St George's Hall in the early 40s before I joined the RAF. I had teamed up with Phil Park in a late night broadcast for the Forces from St Georges. He played the organ and I the piano. I was very sad to hear of the destruction of that beautiful concert hall and beautiful instrument, but also very excited at the prospect of playing the new BBC organ; not least because I had never before played an instrument with five manuals.

A programme I particularly enjoyed playing for was called *Moonlight Lullaby*: a forty-minute sequence of uninterrupted music. Many pleasing items could be performed which might be unsuitable for a morning or midday programme. I was very fond of Coleridge-Taylor's *Three Dream Dances* and his *Scenes from an Imaginary Ballet* and would include one or two of his pieces in a programme together with something like Duke Ellington's *Mood Indigo* or *In a Sentimental Mood*, and perhaps a light ballet item.

All broadcast programmes were live in those days, and there was always an organ-tuner — mechanic in attendance throughout the actual session in case of problems. The man on duty on this occasion, Frank Holden, was a very quiet, pleasant person, yet as I discovered later, one of the most directly outspoken men I have ever met. Throughout the actual broadcast programme, he sat impassively at the far end of the studio, puffing away at his pipe, just listening. As on all previous broadcasts, there was no announcer in the studio and

76

continuity was maintained with Broadcasting House by a system of internal telephones and signal-lights. When I'd finished my programme and the red light had gone out, I turned to Frank, who had been the only other person in the studio with me, and anxiously asked him what he thought. 'Oh,' he replied, 'you'll be back again and pretty soon too I would say; that was very good.' Of course I hardly knew him at the time. But I later learnt that praise from him was praise indeed. He could be, and very often was, scathing in his comments on performers. He heard them all the time.

I also did freelance piano playing in orchestras which existed for the purpose of broadcasting light music. The BBC would engage a fixer to supply a particular orchestra, and he would get together session players, who were very experienced and could play virtually anything at sight. These orchestras and ensembles usually had special arrangements of music which were suitable only for their own combination. Gradually, ensembles came on the air with their own distinctive sound because of their particular combination and arrangements. My own combination of eight musicians was called 'Louis Mordish and his Players'. I led from a Hammond organ and we had our fair share of broadcast programmes such as Music While You Work, Early Morning Music and Late Night Music. I made all the arrangements for this ensemble, as my theatre job left me with free mornings to fit in these other engagements.

I also played solos, including Liszt's *Second Hungarian Rhapsody*, or at least the cadenza, for Sidney Torch and his orchestra. Sidney Torch, a famous organist before the war, became a light-music conductor for the BBC. His orchestral arrangements had the brilliance which characterized his organ playing, and his *Friday Night is Music Night* programmes were outstanding. He was also the conductor of light, popular orchestral works for Columbia Records.

I shall never forget the morning of the recording, a cold day in February. The first half of the morning's session was taken up with the slow first movement in which I did not play a single note. After the coffee break it continued with the second movement, with its famous tune. I sat at a magnificent grand piano, with a microphone suspended over the strings, and rehearsed with the orchestra. During the actual takes, as I followed the score, waiting for my entry, my hands began to shake and my knees trembled as the place for my solo approached. The recording was on wax, and there was no possible way in those days of recording the cadenza separately. Other than at the rehearsal, I'd had no chance to limber up my fingers. I just sat there rubbing my hands. The entry was fast and brilliant with runs from the top end of the keyboard to the bottom and back again, with all sorts of difficult passages to play before the end of the cadenza. I had no doubt that I could play it; the thought running through my mind as I played was that if I made a single mistake, the whole of the movement would have to be recorded again and this might go on and on with the consequent fraying of everyone's nerves, until I got it right.

Harry Fryer died, and was replaced as Musical Supervisor by Felton Rapley, a circuit organist who had the idea of teaming some of us together in stage interludes, like the pre-war days when I was with Sidney Torch and Phil Park. My new colleagues were Bobby Pagan and Terance Casey. We formed *Six Hands in Harmony*, playing three grand pianos. We were a well-rehearsed trio and our act was a triumph. We travelled around the country performing at the larger provincial cinemas, providing pleasing, well staged and entertaining musical programmes. Bobby Pagan and I also performed as a duet. We arranged quite a number of different programmes, which always included a light classical selection and a popular medley. He always played the organ while I was on stage at the grand piano. We toured around the larger cinemas and in the course of our run had many amusing incidents which should never have happened.

There was the one at the Finsbury Park Astoria. After the main film had ended, as usual, the screen tabs closed, the main front curtains came down and the stage was set for our act. Bobby always opened our show by playing some music as he brought the organ up to its pre-arranged level, which was about half-way up so not obscure the piano set centre-stage from the view of the audience. He announced the act from his microphone, then began with the opening bars of the Tchaikovsky Piano Concerto. The stage curtains were still closed, and normally rose as soon as I began playing the big heavy chords; but on this occasion there were no chords – just silence. Bobby, thinking something had delayed me, made a suitably humorous comment and started again. Once more – silence. He made a third announcement, with the same result. What he did not know was that when the film ended the screen, which had to be flown (that is, pulled straight up by stage ropes so that the stage was clear for setting) had caught in some ropes half-way up and was dangling at a dizzy angle. The piano had been placed in position, and the screen lurched perilously just above it. I was sitting at the instrument, ready to start playing, and as I raised my hands to attack the chords, I suddenly became aware of hefty arms and hands from behind shoving the piano away from me. I literally brought my hands down on nothing! The stage director, seeing the dangling screen, realized that not only would it be a laughable stage-setting, but what was worse, it might not even be possible for it to be re-set for the films following our act. That would indeed be a catastrophe. He quickly got assistance and three men just shoved the piano out of the way and began to work furiously to free the screen.

By this time, Bobby was convinced that something really dreadful had happened. He brought the organ up to its full rise level with the stage so that he could explain matters to the audience. The curtains were of course still closed. I in my turn, not knowing what Bobby had done, thought I should go out and explain what had happened, and going through the gap between the curtains, walked straight into the back of the organ. Recovering myself, I went to the left of the organ and began talking at the same time as Bobby, who hadn't seen me. By this time, the audience were laughing uproariously as we each tried in turn to talk to them. Then I heard a voice from behind the curtains: 'You can go ahead with your show now. We've brought the piano right down to the footlights. We'll work on the screen behind the front tabs.'

I disappeared behind the front curtains and took my place on the piano stool, ready to start. Once more Bobby played the opening bars, and this time the audience heard the piano and were treated to the extraordinary sight of the curtains going up a little way, revealing the lower part of the piano and piano stool, both of which were rising, then repeatedly coming down again heavily, going up once more and coming down again.

What had happened was that in the excitement taking place on the stage, the men had just pushed the piano towards the footlights, and somehow the front leg had caught in the curtains. Each time it tried to rise, the piano went with it and being very heavy, was tearing the lining of the curtains. I was trying to play on a leaning piano that kept rising, going down with a crash, then tried to rise again, still leaning at an angle, and coming down again. Finally we had to stop. We were laughing with the audience. I called to the stage hands to come and clear the piano which they did by lifting it bodily from the lining of the curtain (badly torn by now), and putting it down again with both the rear and one of the front legs in the footlights – once again a sloping piano. That was quite an eventful evening.

On another occasion, at a different theatre, the piano was placed on a revolving stage, the idea being that as soon as I started to play, the revolve which had the piano with its small end facing the audience (with myself at the keyboard also facing them) would turn, bringing me and the piano round so that we were in the normal playing position: that is, with my right arm towards the audience. It didn't happen. In the hurry to set the stage, the piano had been placed on the revolve, but not the stool, which had been left on the stage proper. I played the first few chords, the piano on the revolve started to move. But I didn't. So I had to pick up the stool and chase the moving revolve and piano until they came to rest. I continued to play amid tumultuous applause and laughter from the audience.

Amid much professional happiness, my domestic life took a turn for the worse. My wife and I parted. Soon afterwards, my mother died; a very big shock to me, as it was the first death in my family. Because of the domestic situation, I had sent my daughter, Arlene, to a boarding school. I was alone for some years, living for a while with my brother and his family before finding a flat of my own.

One day during her school holidays, Arlene, who was staying with me, said there was a film showing at the Odeon Cinema at Swiss Cottage which she would like to see. I told her that as I knew the manager there, I could arrange for her to see it, take her there and be looked after until I called to collect her. I couldn't stay as I had to play at my own theatre. I phoned the cinema, which was with the same firm, spoke to the manager's secretary and arranged for Arlene to see the film. During my talk to the secretary, she said she knew me, having seen and heard me play at one of the firm's cinemas. We arranged to meet for a coffee. That lady is now my wife! Pearl and I liked each other at sight and my domestic life took a turn for the better straight away – and all this happened because I wanted a free ticket for my daughter to see a film.

Despite the general level of musical excellence, things were not altogether healthy in the cinema world. True, a number of developments took place in the early 1950s, designed to draw in audiences. Screens dramatically increased in width, although the height remained the same. This new shape was called Cinemascope and immediately opened the way to new, spectacular productions. Crowd scenes and pictorial views which previously had been cramped were now seen in natural perspective. Epics began to appear with enormous numbers of people taking part. The first such Cinemascope film was *The Robe* dealing with the crucifixion of Christ.

Another, even more spectacular development was Cinerama, whereby gigantic interlaced screens covered three sides of the cinema, giving the viewer an impression of being present in the scene. Speakers ranged round the hall gave out sound as the action passed that particular point, helping to further the illusion. An arrow shot from a bow would be seen as coming from the front of the screen, then whizz by with the swish given out as it disappeared. People could be heard to talk or sing as they approached from behind, creating an extraordinary feeling of participation. The scenic effects were wonderful, yet Cinerama was a novelty that only lasted a few years. Some cinema screens had a deep frame all around the screen to give an impression of depth to the picture. That didn't last long either. The most important and durable change involved action scenes which for the first time were actually shot outdoors. Previously it had been the custom to build sets in film studios with back-projected scenery. However realistic this appeared, it could only function on a limited scale, and a great deal depended on clever editing.

Nevertheless, throughout the early 1950s, attendances at cinemas began to decline. Television began to erode audience figures, just as later, the craze for Bingo (known before the War as 'Lotto', and played in the Services as 'Housey-Housey') further undermined attendances.

Organists were amongst the first to feel the cold wind of change. Starting with my first appointment after the war at the New Victoria Cinema in late 1945, I was transferred to several other major cinemas on the circuit. Each of these was in a different administrative area, and although I always had a base theatre, such as the Gaumont at Camden Town and then the Gaumont at Chelsea, most of my time was spent playing at different theatres in the London area as a guest organist, the move designed to spread the cost of my princely salary around the circuit rather than have one area only responsible for it. Indeed, there were instances of my being based at a theatre and being there perhaps one week in eight, the rest of the time being spent visiting.

When there was no time for an interlude between films, I supplied link-ups. These were a means of providing continuity in the programme. I picked up the music of the film just ending, obviously in the same key, and modulated into the music of the next film, trying to imitate it in such a way that the audience would not be aware of the change from organ to film music. These organ links also included playing during all periods when the house lights were up: at the end of each complete programme and during ice-cream sales. At the same time, this became a subtle way of phasing out organ interludes as a regular part of the programme, making organists playing for link-ups and providing atmosphere an expensive luxury. With reduced income came cut-throat competition and mergers. My particular firm, the Gaumont British, was in competition with the other two major circuits, the ABC and the Odeon, and for a while retained the very few organists it employed.

Then the Gaumont-British and the Odeon circuit amalgamated to create the Cinema Management Association, or CMA. There were more cinemas to visit as a guest – between six and seven hundred CMA cinemas throughout the country. But only three organists were employed in the West End: Terance Casey at the Gaumont Haymarket; Gerald Shaw at the Odeon Leicester Square; and myself at the Leicester Square Theatre, where I stayed from 1953 to 1958, having been based for fairly lengthy periods at the Trocadero, Elephant and Castle (always associated with the great Quentin Maclean), and the Gaumont-State at Kilburn. In the end, Bobby Pagan left the firm, and the Musical Supervisor's department was dispensed with. Organ interludes became a thing of the past, unable to compete with modern developments. We organists were retained to supply that little extra glamour for special occasions.

Though this was now rather a dull way of earning a living, playing the organ for fill-ins and lights up, it still had its bright spots, with Royal Command first-nights and tours with film artistes to publicise their latest pictures. On one of these tours, I found myself travelling with Joan Collins and Harry Fowler. On another, I was with Inia Te Wiata, the celebrated New Zealand Maori singer and actor. At the firm's expense we had a most enjoyable time travelling around the bigger provincial towns and dining in luxurious and expensive restaurants in London such as *The Mirabelle*. Inia and I became good friends and he often came to my flat to try out songs; visits which I shall always remember, for he had a wonderful bass voice.

At this time, American vocalists still led the pop world. One of the most famous was Johnny Ray, with smash hits *Cry* and *Such a Night*. An English film company had produced a comedy purporting to show the effects on an English family of the visits to them by an American singing star. Jack Buchanan and Thora Hird were the parents, and Janette Scott played the daughter who falls in love with the visitor.

The part of the vocalist was taken by another American star named Jerry Wayne, and my firm thought it would be a good idea to have a personal promotion tour all over the country; he would visit large theatres and industrial firms in order to help publicize the film.

I went as his accompanist. One of the towns we visited was Glasgow. By coincidence, the real Johnny Ray was appearing that week at the local theatre and somebody thought it would be excellent publicity for both these artistes if a meeting between them could be arranged – the real Johnny Ray meeting his film impersonator.

It was a most extraordinary situation. We were all due to meet at a certain time in a special room at one of the hotels. By a strange quirk of fate, as we were actually on our way, everybody involved rounded the corridor corners at the same moment but from opposite ends. We gasped as the two groups walked toward each other – there were only the three of us in our party, but there seemed to be about ten or a dozen or so in Johnny Ray's: his manager, secretary, press agent, musical director, and recording manager.

We had a friendly meeting and were invited to his show. But the next evening we could hardly get in the theatre. The street outside was a solid mass of people; traffic had jammed. It was with the utmost difficulty that we eventually managed to get inside, where we met Johnny Ray and his entourage, saw his act, watched and listened to the hypnotized semi-hysterical audience, and thought: what does it take to make an international star like that?

On two memorable occasions in 1955 and 1956, CMA sent me to Paignton to play for variety seasons at the Odeon Cinema. They were during the summer holiday periods and the management changed from films to live variety to attract an evening audience of holiday makers. I accompanied the acts on the organ, without the assistance

83

of a drummer. It was quite a challenge doing everything on my own, but I had the satisfaction of playing for artistes like Alma Cogan, Dave King, Harry Worth, and the members of the Goon Show: Harry Secombe, Spike Milligan, Michael Bentine and Max Geldray, minus only Peter Sellers. Each artiste played for a week and each season ran for a month. I got on well with all the artistes, with two small exceptions. One was with a certain gentleman who expected me to sound like the London Palladium orchestra – in fact, during the previous few weeks he had been at the Palladium. He was an instrumentalist, and the only parts he gave me for his accompaniment were ordinary manuscript parts used by orchestral pianists in a pit orchestra; just chords with no band figures or any indication of drum rhythms.

After the first show, he asked me to put in some brass figures. After the next, could I add some sax figures? After another, could I also add string passages? On it went until I finally complained that I was composing half his arrangements for him. It was his act, not mine. If he wanted fuller accompaniments, he should have arranged the music himself. He didn't like me a bit after that.

The other exception was very similar. The lady in question, quite a celebrity, brought her own pianist. I did my best to make my very ordinary pit-piano part sound more interesting by adding brass figures, sax figures and string passages without being in any way obtrusive. She knew I was doing a good job because not once was there any adverse comment about my playing. But she was also very aloof and haughty, and refused to acknowledge my existence either on or off-stage.

After the last show on the Saturday night, I was chatting to the manager in his office when a uniformed attendant knocked at the door, saying that the lady wanted to see me: 'She's just given the chief stage-hand 10s., so I wouldn't be surprised if she wants to give you something too.' We met on the theatre gangway. She was holding her arm extended towards me and I could see in her hand an unfolded 10s. note. In very superior tones she offered me the money. I felt insulted. If she thought that all my careful playing and filling-in ideas needed only the same amount of skill as that required by a stage-hand and was therefore worth only 10s., I didn't want it. I refused politely, saying that I didn't take tips, but I would be pleased to have a drink with her whenever convenient, and delighted to buy one in return. I don't think many people had the nerve to talk to her like that, but her condescending manner to musicians made me furious. I did not take the money and I still think my contribution to her act was worth more than 10s. I would have felt better had she offered nothing and genuinely thanked me.

In contrast, there were highly memorable times on the two occasions I was sent from Leicester Square to the Gaumont State at Kilburn to work with visiting American artists.

The first was none other than Bob Hope, who was appearing for a season at the London Palladium. A junior member of the managerial staff decided it would be a marvellous event for the State Cinema if Bob Hope could be persuaded to come along and make a personal appearance. Though the idea was ridiculed he managed to fix it. Word began to spread that Bob Hope would be appearing on the stage one evening. There was absolutely no advertising in case the star failed to turn up. Yet without publicity of any kind, word of mouth was sufficient to bring in the crowds. I was to play the organ and create the atmosphere for the occasion, and when I arrived at the theatre, it was already packed to capacity with all the London management nervously walking around wondering what was going to happen, terribly apprehensive that the young assistant manager had done something which would have dire results.

As the film came to an end tension reached fever-pitch backstage. Like an electrical signal, the message spread that the great man had arrived. I rushed down to the organ and played soft introductory music. Then, when the cue light went on, I launched into *Thanks for the Memory*. The curtains opened and Bob Hope walked on to the stage amid deafening applause. I sat at the organ enjoying the humour. Then he gave me the cue and I started the introduction. He sang several humorous verses and then I nearly fell off the organ seat when I saw him turn, point to me and sing: 'Thanks for the memory. No need to wear a frown, Lou Mordish is in town.' I couldn't believe it: my name mentioned by the great Bob Hope.

On another occasion, my firm decided to present some live shows on Sunday evenings at the Gaumont-State Cinema, and at another very large theatre with the famous American film star Mischa Auer as the star attraction. He was very tall and slim, with large soulful eyes and a pencil-thin moustache. He often played such parts as an eccentric Russian aristocrat or a member of high society. I was to be the musical backing for the whole of the show, and I shall never forget his expression when he arrived at the theatre and learnt that there was no orchestra but just an organ. When he realized that I was to provide the whole of his accompaniment, his eyes seemed to grow even larger and his face registered an expression of utter disbelief.

However, he explained his act to me, which included rolling a couple of oranges on the black keys of the piano which he was playing. The show went on and he appeared, tall and elegant, as the star. When it was all over, I made my way to his dressing-room to see whether he was satisfied with the way I had played his music. At first I didn't see him. Then I became aware of a figure sitting on the floor in a corner of the room, his arms clutching each other round his knees which were drawn up to his chin. He looked up, smiled and said, 'Come in, come in. We paralysed them, you and me together. What a team. Who needs an orchestra. I thanked him saying how much I'd enjoyed accompanying him and how I looked forward to the next occasion. We did one more show together the following Sunday and again he was most complimentary. Somehow, no successful world tour followed. But he certainly was a striking personality and every time I see him on TV in an old Hollywood film, I visualize him sitting on the floor in the corner of his dressing-room with his large, soulful eyes staring up at me.

Around this time I branched into film music. I had a friend named Joe Charman, who was a freelance sound-recording engineer working for film units and travelling all over the world. I'd first met him when I was the organist at the Gaumont State Cinema and he was then the chief projectionist. He was a very able and ambitious young man who did not want to spend the rest of his life just showing films in a cinema. He began studying sound recording and eventually found work in an established film studio. Then he joined forces with a film-editing colleague Bob Bucknell in producing small films for public showing, and they asked me to join in the venture by composing the music.

Accordingly, we put our heads together and produced our first title – a 35 minute short called *His Happy Heath* about the adventures of a small boy spending a glorious, carefree day on Hampstead Heath, concluding in a visit to the fair, with its sideshows and roundabouts. For me, the beauty of the film was that there was no commentary whatsoever, every movement and incident being illustrated by music.

I loved working on it and was thrilled when I was actually recording the music with a very large orchestra in the studio – it all came off. Surely there can be few instances of gratification and pleasure to equal the feelings of someone, whether he is a composer or a playwright, who hears what had been notes or words on paper come to life. I'm fortunate in having experienced this on many occasions – starting so long ago with my *Legend of the Woods* suite. And by one of those extraordinary coincidences, this film was selected to be shown in the same programme as Laurence Olivier's *Richard III* during its long run at the Leicester Square Theatre. Who could wish for a better star-film to help launch a modest short?

In the end, though we made a couple of other films for which I wrote the music, my colleagues could not break through the almost impenetrable barrier of booking agents and circuit bookings. All the same, it had been an exciting experience.

Another pleasant change in my routine work as organist was in the autumn of 1957 when the firm decided to have a season of films of the famous Russian Bolshoi Ballet Company with their star performer Galinova. It was during a period of Anglo-Russian cultural exchanges and we all knew the films were bound to draw very large crowds. One of the top managers in the firm decided to set the scene with the right sort of musical atmosphere, and he asked me to engage an orchestra of twelve musicians who would give a half-hour concert before each showing. It was a marvellous engagement. I had first-class string and woodwind players with piano and percussion. We really gave a miniature concert. I did not play at all but conducted. I walked into the theatre with a spotlight on me, resplendent in tails, proceeded to the orchestra pit, took my place at the rostrum, tapped my baton on the stand and started off with the overture *Susanna's Secret*. The programme was fairly highbrow, including such pieces as Ravel's *Bolero*, Wolf-Ferrari's *Jewels of the Madonna*, Rimsky-Korsakov's *Hymn to the Sun* and *Dance of the Tumblers*. For ten weeks I lived in a musical dream-world. The programme went down well with the audiences. I felt sad when that particular season ended and I went back to filling in on the organ.

With the writing of the film score and the orchestral engagement for the Bolshoi Ballet, I really thought I was now set for the musical highlights of my profession. But it was not to be. Life has a facility for playing odd tricks on people when they're least expecting them.

The first blow fell in June 1958: the death of my father after a stroke. Since the separation of my parents years before, we'd met very infrequently at first, and we were ill at ease together. After the break-up, my mother became very neurotic, and would have turned hysterical if she even suspected I wanted to see him. To this day, I don't know what caused them to separate. I suspect it was because my mother, with her 'small-town', narrow upbringing, was a very jealous person and my father, whom I always remember as a kind, loving man with a sense of humour, resented this.

However, within the last few years I'd seen him more frequently. A previous stroke had already left him slow and ponderous. He could not work. He had remarried, and lived with his second wife in a small flat with just his pension to keep them both going. When I called to see him after an interval of years, he told me that before his first illness, when he could still get around, he would often go to the cinema where I was working, just to see me playing my interlude, when I would bring up the console and talk to the audience. And I never knew he was there sitting among them.

Then, some weeks after my father's death, a letter arrived from Head Office, giving me a month's notice 'owing to the continual and continuing decline in cinema audience attendances'. I was staggered by the news. The letter was apologetic, but it didn't alter the fact that I'd been given the sack – the first time since I was at the Star Cinema at the age of fourteen.

New horizons

I was convinced that my career as a theatre-organist had come to an end, as I had little chance of obtaining an organist's job on another circuit. I'd been one of the last three organists remaining on the CMA circuit – the largest in the country. The only other big firm which used to employ organists, the ABC, had long ago started to dispense with them.

But once again, Providence was on my side. By chance I met an old acquaintance outside the theatre, a music-plugger named Freddy Jones, who worked for one of the many music publishing firms in nearby Tin Pan Alley. (This was a small street off Charing Cross Road, named Denmark Street, where most of the publishers of popular songs and dance music had their offices; most of which have long since disappeared.)

When I mentioned to Freddy what had happened, he asked me if I could play for variety. Of course, I'd had years of experience in that kind of work. It seemed that Delfonts were looking for an organist and Music Director for one of their summer season shows, and Freddy suggested that I write to their Musical Supervisor at the Prince of Wales Theatre. This turned out to be a man named Harold Collins, whom I recognized as the conductor of one of the broadcasting orchestras in which I had played the piano. I didn't know him well as I was always booked for such engagements by a band fixer.

But he was very friendly, and the fact that I had met him so many times certainly made things easier. He said that he knew all he needed to know about me, and offered me the job for the Weymouth summer season. I was elated. Although the engagement wouldn't start until early summer 1959, we discussed terms and details at once. The important thing was that I'd made contact with another firm and there were prospects. Then, to fill in the five months between the end of my theatre-organ job and the start of the summer season, there was another stroke of luck. At this period the Government, to help ease the high unemployment in the entertainment world, had introduced a scheme whereby all promoters of entertainment which included a certain percentage-time of live performers, whether actors, variety artistes or musicians, would be granted a remission in the rate of entertainment tax. Accordingly, some of the larger cinemas in the West End of London began to introduce orchestras to play for a proportion of the programme, giving a popular concert. It was calculated that even with the paying of the salaries of the musicians who were so employed, the savings in tax would be worthwhile and the overall length of the programme would be cheaper than would be the case if a second film had to be hired. Of course, the public need not come in very early to hear the orchestra, which always played at the beginning of each programme; they could always come in to the theatre just before the film started. It was the length of the musical programme not the quality of performance that mattered as regards the remission of tax.

One of these cinemas was the Astoria in Charing Cross Road. The film *Around the World in Eighty Days* was being shown and the conductor of the orchestra, Arthur Anton, was another musician whom I had met at broadcasting sessions. He heard through the grapevine that I would be leaving my theatre and asked whether I'd like to come into his orchestra as organist. I certainly did (I think I was out of work for one week) and stayed there until May 1959.

This was the new pattern of my musical career. Before this I had led a very regular routine sort of life: going to the cinema every day, doing my various stints and returning home at night, just like an office worker. Even the trips I took with Bobby Pagan had become a routine sort of job. But I was now a freelance musician; ready, willing and able to work for anyone or any organisation which would employ me. And the summer show at Weymouth was the first in which I took over the responsibility of accompanying a whole variety show for a season, as distinct from the occasional weekly shows which I had played for CMA in previous years.

Being a Delfont production, the show was bright and sparkling. It starred Bruce Forsyth, who was then riding high, having just completed his first season as compère in *Sunday Night at the Palladium*. It had great supporting acts in the late Gary Miller,

90

Audrey Jeans and other well-known names, with the usual troupe of glamorous dancers in the Tiller Girls. We gave two shows every evening and although the weather was marvellously hot and dry – just what holiday-makers were looking for – we played to capacity houses.

At the end of the summer season, I returned to London and continued my freelancing, filling in the weeks with recording sessions and broadcasting until the end of December, when I joined Henry Croudson, the organist at the Empire Cinema Leicester Square, in a musical presentation which took place just before the showing of the film *Ben Hur*. We had the assistance of a percussionist who spread all his instruments as far as he could across the centre of the stage. Xylophone, vibraphone, tubular bells, timpani and normal drum kit gave the impression of a large orchestra. Henry was on the extreme left at the organ console, the drummer Cyril Holdsworth in the centre, and I on the extreme right at a grand piano. This musical presentation, which included all the Hebrew music Henry could find, was not only intended to set the scene for the film, but was also part of the whole programme; live entertainment, thus qualifying for a remission in the tax rate. Even though there were only three of us in the presentation in this giant super cinema, our programme went down well with the audience and I was sorry when this engagement came to an end.

Again my good luck held. I joined the Victoria Palace orchestra as Hammond organist under the baton of a very old friend, Jack Ansell, whom I'd met years ago as a friend of David Greenbaum. The show which was then running was *The Clown Jewels*, with the Crazy Gang. Funny, spectacular, very bright and colourful, it didn't flag for a moment. One of the memorable highlights was the staging of the song 'Strolling', which was sung by Flanagan and Allen with the entire cast, all dressed in tails and toppers, joining in the song in a very gentle strolling routine.

There was also the Royal Command Variety Show held that year at the Victoria Palace. Among the many famous names who appeared that night were four Americans: Nat King Cole, Sammy Davis Junior, John Horton (an actor who was in a very successful TV serial) and Liberace. Everybody had heard about the legendary Liberace, with his flamboyant clothes, candelabra and lace cuffs. When he appeared at the rehearsal, all smiles as usual, I must confess to being somewhat prejudiced. But when he played through a Liszt rhapsody, and played it extremely well, he could wear whatever he wished as far as I'm concerned, because he was a very good pianist with an ability to sell. Not just a showman.

Then back to Weymouth for another season, with Anne Shelton and a very young Morecambe and Wise in supporting roles. I was in Weymouth again in December to play for a pantomime starring Ronnie Ronalde, at that time a famous whistler. In his solo spot he would sing a popular song and whistle the second chorus; his pièce de résistance was *In a Monastery Garden*, where he introduced a variety of bird whistles. The audience loved it.

I was discovering that in the world of freelancing, contacts rather than ability were the road to professional success. In particular, powerful fixers were able to provide any type of musical combination required for any particular purpose such as an orchestra for the recording of film music, special combinations for recording and backing purposes of popular music, or orchestras for theatre and musical shows. Quite a number of able and experienced musicians were unable to find work in these fields because they had fallen foul of these fixers. This was the case principally with string-players, of whom there was always an abundance. How these fixers started on their careers has always been something of a mystery, but quite a few of them (who were usually also string-players) did very well out of these engagements, for in addition to supplying the required orchestra, they invariably fixed themselves in their own instrumental sections. Some whom I happened to hear playing on their own were unbelievably ordinary, but they were experts at marshalling other peoples' talents.

Of course, freelancing presented its own challenges. I never knew beforehand what I might have to play. I recall one broadcasting session where the conductor had included as one of the items in his programme a piano solo which at first glance petrified me. I'd never seen or heard of this particular piece before; it was a very fast, rhythmic number in Latin American rhythms and with orchestral counter-melodies. It was so busy that to play it you had to look at the keyboard all the time. I complained to the conductor about playing it at sight (like so many band-leaders he was a violinist, and knew very little about the piano). 'What's the problem?' he replied. 'All the notes in the music are on the keyboard, aren't they?'

Somehow I floundered through it at rehearsal. During the coffee-break, when everyone went out of the studio for about fifteen

92

minutes, I set to work on the piece, committing the awkward florid passages to memory and generally learning the shape. Thank goodness for that break and for the few minutes rest before the live transmission when I could try it over again and again. Happily, all went well and afterwards everybody congratulated me, but it was certainly a challenging morning.

The BBC engaged me as an extra for their programme *Grand Hotel* which broadcast live every Sunday. The orchestra, under the leadership of Reg Leopold, one of the most experienced violinists in the profession, included the famous cellist Reg Kilbey. Both of these musicians were absolutely first class in the world of light music. The pianist was also a very old friend of mine, Teddy Rubach, and the whole ensemble, consisting of nine players, performed the specially arranged music in a superb manner. It was a joy to be part of that group. Originally, I played the Mustel organ, a kind of harmonium, but then switched to the celesta, and on occasions when we played something like the Intermezzo from *Cavalleria Rusticana* or *The Lost Chord*, I played the concert organ, which was within easy reach.

I stayed with this ensemble on a freelance basis for many years, commuting on the Sundays when I was away on summer season engagements and was not required for a Sunday concert. When Teddy Rubach died, I took over the piano with the ensemble. This was indeed a challenge as in addition to playing the normal orchestral items, many of which had been arranged by that brilliant hotel-music pianist Jack Byfield, there were always the accompaniments to the violin solos and vocal solos and sometimes even a piano solo; all of which were part of the fixed pattern of that particular programme, and demanded a good technique and sympathetic playing.

The summer season of 1961 found me in Weymouth yet again. The star of the show was Vic Oliver, a man who had been a legendary figure in the world of entertainment since his youngest days. He was tall and sophisticated, with an unusual accent which helped add point to his stories. He had originally come from Austria, settled in America, and among other events in his crowded life, married Winston Churchill's daughter Sarah. His act was very polished and included violin and pianos solos; altogether, he had tremendous class, a quality which enabled him to play at some of the world's leading theatres.

When the show had been running for some time and had settled into a comfortable routine, I thought I would add a little impromptu music to part of his act. I'd noticed that in between his stories he would quietly play a few bars of music on the violin he always carried with him. During one such violin interlude, a Hungarian piece which I knew quite well, I very quietly began to play an accompaniment. He was standing centre-stage, very close to the footlights; I was sitting at the organ immediately below, looking up at him. I noticed his eyes drop down as he glanced at me, but he made no other sign and continued playing. For the next house he played a different tune and I crept in quietly once again. This time I noticed a faint smile, and thereafter he played lots of different tunes, mostly continental, smiling a little as though to say, 'I wonder if you know this one?' Which I usually did. After that, we would often have little chats about music and became quite friendly; as friendly, that is, as a former Prime Minister's son-in-law could be with an organist in a summer show. Indeed, after that summer season, he gave me quite a number of engagements as accompanist to very well-known artistes and I appeared with him in some of his own shows.

The next visit to Weymouth was for the pantomime *Dick Whittington*, but I shall always remember it for a very different reason. Quite a few of the cast stayed at the same boarding house. The landlady, who was Swiss, decided to give us all a special treat. We sat at our tables speculating what this could be. She walked into the room, beaming and holding a large tray covered by a serviette. A pungent aroma was noticeable. 'There you are, a special treat for you all. I made it myself – jugged hare.' One by one we all politely refused it. As each in turn offered some excuse her expression changed. Her lips set into a thin line. By the time the last person had refused, she was pale with anger. She swept out of the room and during the rest of the time we stayed at her house, none of us saw her again. She was furious; and although she prepared our meals as arranged, all the waiting at table was done by her husband, who likewise remained silent and unsmiling – though whether from remorse or from his wife's anger nobody could tell.

In 1962 I was engaged by another management for the summer season at Clacton. Top of the bill was the irrepressible Billy Cotton and his band. We had weekly changes of supporting acts. One of them was Mrs Mills, who was retained for a second week and although pleased at the news was upset because she only had one routine. She came to me for help to put another routine together. She was delighted with my advice, and I was very pleased when I saw how well this went with the audience.

After the usual post summer-season freelancing, I was offered a job to play entr'acte music on a Hammond organ at the Duchess Theatre, where Irene Handl was appearing in a comedy called *Good-Night, Mrs Puffin*. This was mainly an evening show, so I had plenty of time for other engagements. This particular play was very successful and included a transfer to the Duke of York Theatre. My engagement ran from September 1962 to February 1963. No need to go away from home for pantomime that year. The only sadness during the engagement was the death of my brother Jack, who died very suddenly after a short illness.

By now I had acquired a family, Valerie and Simon, and we had moved to Wembley Park. (At this time Arlene was living with her mother.) My family came with me each summer when I went away for the season. We packed the car with everything we might need, locked the house doors and disappeared for the duration, when we were more or less on holiday the whole of the time, whatever the weather.

Summer 1963 saw us at Southsea again for Bernard Delfont, where the stars of the show were Arthur Askey with Mike and Bernie Winters. Then Weymouth again at Christmas for *Cinderella*, which ran for seven weeks.

For summer 1964 I went to Bournemouth for a new management, George and Alfred Black, noted for their very lavish West End shows. I conducted an orchestra of fourteen musicians, with no playing whatsoever. Definitely a step up. I had saxes, brass and rhythm sections, and I enjoyed being in charge of such a well-sounding orchestra. It was a great season. The stars were Matt Monro and the Dallas Boys, with very strong supporting acts. The whole of the production took place on what was really an open concert platform, the Winter Gardens being the home of the Bournemouth Symphony Orchestra. There were no curtains or tabs, back cloths, sets or drapes and everybody in the show had to come on to the platform – I can hardly call it a stage – and leave it in full view of the audience. The orchestra was in tiers on one side of the stage.

On the Sundays, the management presented an entirely different show at the Pier Pavilion: *The Music of Ivor Novello*. This had a variety of artistes, many of whom were famous for their association with that gifted song writer; names such as Barry Sinclair, Olive

Gilbert and Margaret Burton. For this I played the Hammond organ, providing the musical accompaniment with the assistance of the band pianist, Reg Farrow.

I found the air at Bournemouth very relaxing, and have to confess that on occasions the atmosphere, coupled with the heat of the hall, had a soporific effect when I was conducting. I really had to work hard to avoid dozing off not only during the comedian's patter, but whenever I was not actually waving the baton.

Soon after the Bournemouth season had closed, a new strand was added to my professional life in a most unusual way. I found myself in a beautifully furnished flat in Charles Street off Berkeley Square, talking to a man named George Frazer. He was writing music for a new pantomime called *Give a Dog a Bone* at the Westminster Theatre, and was looking for a Musical Director. It was being written, produced and presented by Moral Rearmament, a group that was trying to help people alter their lives according to its own strong religious convictions. Though it all sounded very strange to me, the job sounded interesting musically, so I took on the role of MD.

My first task was to write proper piano parts for the melodies which George Frazer composed – tuneful if somewhat old-fashioned in style. Then rehearsals began. The producer was a well-known actor called Henry Cass, and the choreographer Bridget Espinoza, who had been a famous ballerina. We discovered that the only music for the show was the songs that George Frazer had written; there were no production scenes or dancing sequences envisaged in the original script. So the three of us, Henry, Bridget and I, had to create these situations. It seemed that the original idea of the author and the composer was to have the characters in the play just stand and sing their songs as they occurred in the course of the story – with all their many verses – so that their message could get across.

Henry was in despair. How could he produce a production scene when there isn't one to produce? He decided to add lines, build up situations and scenes together with Bridget's ideas. I adapted and arranged the music accordingly. By the time we had it ready for presentation, the show was quite different. Somebody had given the management the idea that the ideal orchestral accompaniment for this pantomime would be a quartet: Hammond organ, guitar, drums and trumpet. I thought it a very peculiar line-up and tried in vain to persuade them not to have a trumpet: it would stand out like a sore thumb.

The message of rigid ideas and beliefs that MRA wanted to give the world made the panto unlike any I've ever seen before or since. There was no girl-boy romance, no comedy scenes, no 'Dame' or audience participation. It was not a panto at all in the conventional meaning of the word, but rather a musical-playlet, with a message of good triumphing over evil, portrayed by a King Rat. It is not for me to comment on the beliefs and teachings of MRA, but it would appear that if one went through life not being greedy and being courteous as the occasion arose, all would be well.

Still, I must say the Westminster Theatre management were very good and considerate employers, and the theatre itself was pleasant to work in. They obviously liked my work because quite early during the run of the panto, they invited me to come back the following Christmas, and in fact I played for the same pantomime, *Give a Dog a Bone*, for no fewer than eleven seasons – from 1964 to 1974 inclusive – a most pleasant and comfortable series of engagements, and all in London. And in the end I did persuade them to substitute a tenor saxophone doubling clarinet for the trumpet, a much better sound in a small place.

Soon after the show opened I had to play for a pantomime in Stockton. What a difference. It was held in a cinema seating 3000. There was lavish spectacle with brilliant costumes and any amount of comedy and music. It starred Al Read, The Seekers and Ronnie Carroll; all of them very popular artistes who were frequently on radio and TV with their own series. I did no playing, but instead conducted the very large pit orchestra which gave out a much more conventional theatre-orchestra sound than the quartet I had just left. This production had all the normal pantomime ingredients; virtually everything the Westminster show tried to avoid.

In the spring of 1965 Bob Bucknell, one of my old friends with whom I had collaborated in film-making, approached me with a new idea. He was a film-editor and had contacts with companies which produced records of background music. These were publishers who commissioned composers to write all types of music which could help set the atmosphere and mood of a film or play. These pieces of music were especially useful for documentary films, travelogues and news-reels, and could be used for an enormously varied number of situations such as sporting events, races, natural disasters, riots, comedy, tragedy, eastern, western, modern and period music.

His plan was to combine forces in the mood-music world: I would write the music and he would bring these pieces to the attention of his colleagues. In fact I'd already written a number of mood-music compositions for various publishers, and knew the sort of thing required: music to be played at sight and easy enough to be rehearsed and recorded in a few sessions. I agreed to Bob's suggestion and set to work composing and orchestrating quite a number of different types of suitable pieces. My experience years ago as a pianist in the days of silent films now came in very useful and I wasn't worried about the mechanics of writing. I'd already had quite a number of my compositions and arrangements played over the years.

But there was one problem. At that period, the Musicians' Union forbade its members to record for mood-music libraries. It was feared that if such recordings did take place, there would eventually be so much recorded music available that the service of live musicians would no longer be required. So music publishers took their work to countries like Holland, France or Germany where no bans existed and had their music recorded there. Indeed, the Musicians' Unions in those countries probably welcomed these sessions as they brought work to their members.

Through the good offices of a friend named Albert Gordon who was living outside Stuttgart with his German wife, we contacted a fixer who played with the Stuttgart Radio Orchestra and arranged a two-day recording session at a studio with an orchestra, a musical director and sound engineers. I worked hard at my music, and in due course sent the scores to the conductor. Then Bob and I decided to go there ourselves and have a look at the set-up, as he was technically-minded and wanted to ensure that everything would be in order. It was quite an experience. We flew out to Stuttgart, and visited the recording studio and the radio station where we met the fixer and the conductor. The recording sessions were successful. I sat in the control room, listening and passing on comments to the conductor in my limited, halting German. Fortunately, my friend's wife, who spoke fluent English, came along with us and helped to translate.

On this and subsequent recording trips I became aware of the wonderful international language of music, and its power to draw people together. On one expedition our return journey took in

Heidelberg and Bonn. I was thrilled to go to Beethoven's birthplace and see his walking sticks, ear trumpets, scores and the piano on which he played. They made me realize that he was a human being, not just a name.

On another occasion we took our caravan, and made a holiday of the trip. We were travelling late at night, making our way towards the next big town, where we hoped to find accommodation. (We had no fixed schedule and never booked ahead.) My son Simon, who was only a few years old, was very tired, and I thought it best to put him to bed in the caravan.

It was very dark and we were travelling along a country road when I noticed a car pass me, and stop some way ahead. Then a red lamp was swinging backwards and forwards. I continued driving, not knowing what was intended. Again the car passed me and stopped with the red lamp still swinging. I stopped and saw two policemen approach, tall and blond in their German uniforms, and looking as if they had stepped out of a film. They fired many questions at me. When I answered in faltering German, one of the policemen broke into excellent English, saying he'd noticed someone in the caravan and didn't I know it was forbidden in Germany? I did not know, as the only experience I'd had in towing a caravan was last year on our previous visit. When I explained that my little son was asleep and my wife was staying with him he said, 'Well, you can't leave them there while you drive. Where are you staying tonight?' I told him we'd made no arrangements, and were looking for an hotel or an inn. We were told to bring Pearl and Simon into the car and wait. The two policemen returned to their vehicle and five minutes later told us that using their radio they'd found accommodation for us at an inn.

So we followed them for some miles along country roads and suddenly found ourselves coming to a brightly lit building outside which the landlord and his wife were waiting for us. It was wonderful to see such an inviting, comfortable place, and after thanking the two policemen we made our way inside and were shown our rooms. After putting the children to bed, my wife and I made our way downstairs where we enjoyed a meal served by a smiling host and hostess – just like in a story book. I noticed a Hammond organ in the room. I pretended not to know what it was and the landlord explained that he played on it a little for his own and his customers' entertainment. 'I can play a little,' I said. 'Can I try it out and see how I like it?'

I began to play. There were looks of astonishment on the faces of everyone present. I stopped and told them that I really knew what it was, and began playing every German tune I could think of, including music from *The Merry Widow* and Strauss waltzes. The audience was beaming. My stock was very high and I'm sure I forged a strong link in Anglo-German relations. It was altogether a most pleasant evening – thanks to the two policemen!

Summer 1965 found me once again at Bournemouth, the stars this time being Kathy Kirby and Russ Conway. The Sundays were again devoted to shows at the Pier Pavilion and that year the theme was 'Songs from the Shows', with Jessie Matthews as the attraction. Again I was assisted by Reg Farrow with whom I had established a strong musical rapport. My family was with me for the whole season; we rented a flat which became our home from home for almost three months. The only unhappiness during this season was the deaths within a few weeks of my father-in-law and my former wife.

After a winter run of *Give a Dog a Bone*, I returned to Bournemouth for the summer season of 1966, still for the same management but this time at the Pavilion Theatre with Harry Worth (whom I had first met years before at Paignton), Billy Dainty, an up-and-coming young impressionist named Mike Yarwood, and Joe Henderson with, of course, excellent supporting acts and dancers. The show ran into the beginning of October, with the Ivor Novello programme of two years previously repeated on Sundays. Again, I did no playing. Conducting seemed to have become the normal thing for me at summer shows.

One of the producers at Bournemouth was Stanley Willis-Croft, a highly respected professional, very experienced and imaginative. He was approached by the management of the Cliffs Pavilion Theatre at Westcliff, near Southend, to produce their forthcoming summer show and asked me to come along as his Musical Director. The management had been very disappointed with previous productions, although they had always paid whatever the impresario had asked for. They felt they were not getting fair value for their outlay, not knowing how much was spent on artistes and production and how much went into the producer's pocket, a not unknown happening in show business. This time, the management decided they themselves would book the artistes and be responsible for all expenses so that the Civic Corporation would know exactly where their money went.

The venue was near London, and if the show went well, I might be asked to return, so I went along to meet the management. I was not required to play anything, but sat in a corner of the room listening to people singing or dancing their audition pieces to a piano accompaniment. The two members of the management sat at a table, with Stanley at the far end of the room making notes and having little consultations from time to time, talking to various artistes and generally being very business-like. When the auditions had finished, I went over to the table and shook hands with Stanley. He introduced me to Les Cullen, who was the manager of the theatre, and to his colleague, who was the Director of Amenities for the corporation. We had a friendly talk. Les praised my work at Bournemouth. At the end of our discussion, I left the room as the appointed Musical Director for the forthcoming summer show, a position I was to hold for eight consecutive summer seasons from 1967 to 1974.

That first summer season was a triumph. Stanley had some wonderful ideas about staging. The show was colourful, spectacular and entertaining. As it was in the nature of an experiment, the council would not commit itself beyond a certain budget and could not therefore afford a star name. But it did have as top of the bill one of the funniest entertainers I have ever seen: Billy Dainty, an absolute natural. As Stanley had foreseen, we were both asked to work again at the Cliffs Pavilion. We found Les Cullen to be most helpful and co-operative; and indeed, he and I became very good friends. The choreographer was a young man named Tommy Shaw who had some really good modern dance ideas, for which I wrote original music. He would describe his basic concepts, illustrate them with dance movements and I would improvise on the piano waiting for his comments. I'd make quick musical notes and gradually work out a piece of music, to which he then set a routine. It was an exhilarating experience.

During my third year at the Cliffs Pavilion Stanley Willis-Croft died after a short illness. As Tommy had already discussed the production with Stanley he took over as producer as well as being choreographer and the show went ahead. There were no names in the production that year. But the year after, 1970, with Les Cullen promoted to Director of Amenities, the management decided that they would make their summer shows priority productions and engage 'names'. Accordingly, for the forthcoming season, the top act was a group of young men called The Dallas Boys, whom I had previously met at Bournemouth. Vocalists and comedy impressionists, they were extremely popular at that time. With their high-powered, forceful act and the support of the talented artistes on the bill, the show provided excellent entertainment.

Many people believe in luck, fate, or providence. I've wondered so many times what sort of professional life I would have had if I had not as a very young man accepted that engagement at the Marlborough Theatre, Holloway, where I was asked to 'jazz it up, son, jazz it up'. I am the first to admit to my own good fortune and have often thought of the way my professional career developed through chance meetings or contacts. Chief of these was Van Dam. The arrangements I wrote for him led to my engagement as pianist by Joseph Muscant for the famous Commodore orchestra at Hammersmith. Later, he persuaded me to become a theatre organist with all its subsequent changes and re-arrangements of my professional life; and again he persuaded me to volunteer for the RAF during the War, saving me from work in the Army Pioneer Corps, where my hands might have been ruined by the heavy manual work. From this came my subsequent re-engagement as organist by the firm of Gaumont-British Cinemas, with whom I stayed until 1958, and my meeting with Freddy Jones which led me to work with Delfont's Musical Advisor, and my engagements with that firm for summer seasons and pantomimes. There were also my eight summer seasons at Westcliff, my eleven pantomime seasons at the Westminster Theatre, and the other prouctions for which I also acted as Musical Director: *Annie* (not the American comic character but the story of one of MRA's devoted workers), and *GB*, a political revue. I mention all this because during the seasons at Westcliff when I met and played for many well-known and even famous names in the variety world, and also met Dickie Henderson. He was one of the big names in show business, and the man who, though I did not know it at the time, was responsible for another major development in my career.

Musical Director

Though I'd seen Dickie Henderson in West End productions such as *The Teahouse of the August Moon* and *Wish You Were Here*, it was not until 1971 that I got to know him well.

It was towards the end of the season, when we had a special midnight matinée show in aid of a charity, with many visiting stars taking part. During the afternoon, when we were rehearsing, there was a lull, and while we waited I began to play very quietly a classical piano work, purely for my own entertainment. Someone said, 'Louis, why don't you play a proper classical solo tonight? Everyone thinks you can only play show-biz music, so play something really good and surprise them all.' Then, that night, just before the concert started, the stage-manager said to me, 'Louis, during the acts when the artistes have their own pianists and you have to leave the instrument, just stand at the side of the stage; don't leave it during the acts.' I thought it a strange request, but did as I was asked.

The artiste in question was Eartha Kitt. She finished her act and walked off with her pianist as Dickie returned to the stage. I thought he was going to introduce the next act, but instead he said, 'And now Ladies and Gentlemen, I'd like to present someone who doesn't know he's going to come on stage; he doesn't know what this is all about. Louis Mordish, will you please come here and join me.'

I was flabbergasted. My first thoughts were that I was going to be asked to play a piano solo. I felt upset and angry because I didn't relish the idea of having to perform something without proper preparation. I joined him at the microphone. 'Louis,' he said, 'since you came into the theatre to-day, something has happened which will alter your life. You didn't know it earlier, but you will know it now. Louis, you've become a grandfather!' I was presented with a bottle of champagne, amid the cheering of the crowded house. There can't have been many occasions in the history of entertainment when a man

103

has been informed in the presence of more than a thousand people that he has become a grandfather. My elder daughter Arlene had married a young scientist named John Haigh and I knew that a 'happy event' was fairly imminent. My wife had phoned the theatre, asking them to pass on the good news. The management passed the information on to Dickie, and between them they'd arranged the announcement on-stage. I was overwhelmed, couldn't believe I was actually a grandfather, but very relieved that I wasn't asked to play a piano solo!

Towards the end of the season, Dickie asked me whether I'd like to accompany him on some one-night cabaret dates. I agreed willingly. His previous accompanist, Paul Burnett, had taken over the position of Musical Supervisor for Bernard Delfont on the death of Harold Collins. This left Dickie without a pianist and MD. He went on to offer me more dates so that, in effect, I became his Musical Director. As usual, I continued to play for my regular panto at the Westminster Theatre, and in between the end of that season and the next summer season at Westcliff, I played for all of Dickie's dates in addition to the regular freelance work which usually took place in the mornings.

The stars of 1972 at Westcliff were Leslie Crowther and John Hanson. The producer was once again Tommy Shaw. I always enjoyed the pre-production meetings, usually held at Tommy's house, when the principal artistes and Les Cullen would discuss with him their respective ideas for the show. As MD I would join in with my comments. It was always interesting to work on the various suggestions, adding further ideas, moulding and shaping the plans until one could almost see the end product. Often as not, when these ideas were being rehearsed, alterations and adaptations had to be made until everyone was satisfied with the results. Then would come the opening night with its heady atmosphere and last minute checking.

The 1972 season was highly enjoyable, and Leslie was a very co-operative artist. As the star of the show, he always appeared for his own act as the last performer in the programme, although he had already appeared several times in various items and sketches previously. He quickly realized that if he went on for too long, the musicians would be in danger of missing their last train back to London. It was not uncommon for him, about half-way through his act, to ask those in the orchestra pit 'Are we alright tonight, chaps?'; and depending on our answer, he would obligingly cut some gags. At the end of the performance, the musicians, myself included, rushed like mad from the pit, snatched our hats and coats from the band-room and left the non-commuters to pack away their colleagues' instruments.

After that summer season there were only a few weeks to fill in before the start of rehearsals for the panto *Give a Dog a Bone* at the Westminster Theatre. Although most of the artists had already appeared in this show, and the script and music were identical each year, the principals were usually new. The management was always friendly and the engagement a pleasant one, but sometimes one or two of the performers would be upset when they received 'notes' from the higher-ups in the movement asking them to put more 'feeling' and 'sincerity' in the words of their songs. They were told that the meaning of the lyrics was more important than the tune. Indeed, I was asked more than once as MD to have a talk with the artists and persuade them to 'put the message of the words more forcibly across to the audience'. I would dutifully have a chat as requested, but the usual reply was: 'What more can I do? I'm trying my best. I can't be expected to believe all that stuff. I'm an actor, not a missionary!'

After the 1973 panto finished, the management presented a revue called *GB* (standing for Great Britain). I was engaged as MD. It was not really a revue as most people understand the word. Although it contained music (some of which, written by another member of their movement, was delightful) and sketches, every item contained a 'message' either semi-religious or political. The MRA hated the political left, and was very anti-communist. There was very little real humour: the movement was a very solemn one and if I dare say it, did not possess a sense of the ludicrous or absurd. Some of the lighter items were quite witty and clever, but in all the years I worked for them and in all the shows I saw at the theatre, not once can I recall hearing the audience really laugh. Everything seemed so solemn, the humour so genteel and respectable. But they were good employers and kind to the artists and musicians, establishing a pleasant atmosphere with excellent back-stage conditions.

In the spring of that year came the first of many trips abroad with Dickie. He phoned one day to ask whether I'd like to go with him to Australia for a five-week engagement. I couldn't believe it. The furthest I'd ever flown was to Stuttgart. I asked to think it over, but everybody told me I'd be mad if I even thought of turning down this opportunity. It was the chance of a lifetime to go to the other side of the world. The Westminster Theatre management very kindly released me from *GB* for about six weeks, and so one April morning at 2 am, I boarded a Qantas Boeing 747 at Heathrow to join Dickie and his wife Gwyneth 'down under'.

The plane journey in itself was an adventure. We touched down at Athens, Bahrain and Singapore, all extremely exotic sounding places. And as I walked around these airports, I felt sure these were all film sets and the people about me all film extras dressed up in various national costumes. On arrival at Sydney airport, I sent a cable home informing my family I'd reached Australia safely. After collecting my luggage, I took a taxi to the hotel where accommodation had already been arranged for me. I was now definitely a world traveller.

The first thing I noticed, understandably, was the sunshine. Most of the time the weather was perfect. We played at the St George's League Club, one of the largest clubs in Sydney, and an enormous place with every kind of entertainment available for its members. It was not only a social club but also a sports club. There was practically every indoor sporting facility one could wish for, and five restaurants ranging from full à la carte service to gigantic snack bars. There were also several dance floors with different bands catering for different dancers according to their age-group. There was a theatre and club rooms, and any number of different types of bars, including a piano bar and a multitude of 'one-armed bandits'. A fantastic place.

It was a wonderful season. Dickie already had friends there, and we had a most enjoyable social life. We were taken to various places around Sydney, and to some excellent restaurants where we dined at night in the open air. One of the highlights of our visit was a trip round Sydney Harbour in a little launch which was almost swamped by the waves. We all held on to the rails of the boat like grim death, giving each other sickly smiles and pretending to enjoy it. There were a few anxious moments when Dickie's yachting hat fell into the water at a spot marked *Danger – sharks* and he leant overboard to retrieve it.

I also renewed acquaintanceship with a very old friend, John Addess, who had emigrated with his family soon after the War. We were brought up together. Our parents had known each other since

106

they were *landsleit* in Russia, and had continued their friendship until the ends of their lives. We hadn't met for over twenty years. It was a very emotional reunion.

Back home again, I resumed the engagement at the Westminster Theatre, which finished just before the beginning of the Westcliff summer season. This was very much the same as in previous years, the star this time being Harry Worth and the producer Tommy Shaw. There was really nothing new to expect in my seventh consecutive season: music, dancing, comedy and sketches in different forms and guises. I'm inclined to think that the old saying is very true that there's nothing really new in show business.

Meanwhile, though there were fewer organ broadcasts than before, I continued to record, usually from the Gaumont State Cinema in Kilburn, for the programme entitled *The Organist Entertains*, which at that time was produced and presented by Robin Richmond. For each session I recorded six or seven items which were mainly transcriptions of light orchestral works: Dvorak's *Slavonic Dances*, a popular overture or a couple of movements from an orchestral suite such as Bizet's *L'Arlésienne* or the ballet music from *William Tell*. Robin would never allow me to play other types of music. 'I've got any number of organists on my books who can play *Sleepy Lagoon* or rhythm numbers old or new,' he would say, 'but only three who can play the sort of music I need to balance my programmes. You're one of them, so keep on playing the good stuff!'

The following summer season at Westcliff was sadly the last. The stars this time were my old friends Billy Dainty and Ted Hockridge, well-known from many West End musicals. By way of a change, the producer and choreographer was Lionel Blair, Tommy Shaw having taken up a permanent position with a ballet company. The decision to discontinue summer shows was for a very good reason: not enough people were coming in during the season, despite the quality of the performances. Westcliff and Southend were no longer holiday seaside towns to which people would come during the summer; they were too near London. Many residents were now commuters, making these places suburbs. If they wanted to go to the theatre they would stay in town after work and visit one of the many shows available. Thereafter the policy was altered to have one-nighters with famous names, or a visiting weekly play or musical. They didn't require a resident summer orchestra.

1974 also saw the last season of the pantomime *Give a Dog a Bone*. It had been running for ten years and this would be its eleventh production. The directors of MRA came to the conclusion that the show was too costly to keep presenting. It was the old story: declining audiences, not least because most people were looking for entertainment, not something which preached a message.

After that last season, I continued to play for Dickie. One of the most pleasant engagements was a visit to Baden-Baden, where he was to take part in a TV show to celebrate the international nature of the cabaret artistes appearing at the famous casino. Dickie represented the English-speaking world, even though for one of his songs he sang a special German version. The whole visit was memorable. We both fell in love with the elegance of the town. It was easy to imagine the gentry and aristocrats who used to visit the spa. The orchestra was made up of Germans and Czechs. They all spoke English, and were excellent musicians. After the show, everybody who had taken part travelled in a convoy for a magnificent evening at a mountain inn. There were log timber-walls, ceilings, fireplaces and tables.

One incident in particular stayed in my memory. One of the acts was a vocal male quartet who sang in the American style, obviously modelling themselves on some of the leading American groups. I noticed one of them was wearing a Star of David. When I asked him why, he replied that his father was Jewish, and had died when he was a child. Though he knew very little about the Jewish way of life he was deeply drawn to anything which he felt concerned the Jewish faith. In my struggling German – liberally helped out with Yiddish – I answered all his questions to the best of my ability and felt that I had done something worthwhile in helping him in his quest.

Two other trips abroad come to mind. One was to Naples, where we were to perform in the NATO Officers' Club, an engagement memorable for an illustration of how-not-to-run-an-airline.

We had to change planes at Milan. But with wonderful inefficiency our plane was taking off as we arrived. There was chaos, with officials running round frantically and fierce arguments between passengers and airport staff. (It was one of the very few occasions when I saw Dickie lose his temper.) A long queue of angry passengers, including some high-ranking NATO officers, was besieging an harassed official behind a desk. He suggested that we take an overnight train from Milan to Naples. However, seats could not be guaranteed. We might have to stand all the way and pay our own fare. Alternatively, we could hire a taxi. A short, swarthy man offered to take us. Dickie took one look at him and decided that he looked like a brigand who would hold us to ransom in the mountains. Then the poor official who was being harassed finally relented and arranged accommodation for us and a first flight out the next morning. We were all furious. But imagine our surprise when we pulled up at a really magnificent hotel called *Principe e Savoia*. I had a most magnificent suite to myself. Dickie and I dined in a very elegant restaurant with service as only the Italians know how. We were glad we'd avoided the brigand's taxi!

Naples was fascinating. Like all tourists, we took a trip to Pompei. Fortunately for us it was not crowded with visitors as we were there out of season. Another trip was to Capri, where we visited the famous Blue Grotto, which is entered by a small opening in the cliff face. To do this, we first had to change from a launch onto a small rowing boat. Then, just as we entered the opening, we had to lie flat on our backs while the oarsman gave a tremendous pull and the boat glided through into the cave. The water there is light blue in colour because of the presence of mineral deposits. It was a strange feeling to be in that dark cavern watching the entrance hole getting smaller and smaller as we were rowed about in darkness.

I hardly had time to pause for breath after the final panto performance at the Westminster Theatre in February 1975 before I was on my way with Dickie to Nairobi in Kenya. The engagement was for a month at the famous New Stanley Hotel, where we were given VIP treatment. After each night's performance, we would be invited to join a party, usually at the bar, where we passed the time in most agreeable company. Many of the locals were English employees of big organisations who had gone to Kenya on two-year contracts. They had a very high standard of living, resided in beautiful homes and had local staff to do the housework. It seemed the only work done by the wives of these ex-patriots was to decide on next day's dinner menu. All the cooking and housework was done by their 'boys' and 'girls'.

Despite my orthodox Jewish upbringing, I found that as the years went by I became less and less observant of the traditional customs and practices of the faith. I had long ceased attending on High

Festival days, and have ceased to observe the strict dietary laws regarding kosher food, although there are still many things, shellfish for instance, which I cannot easily bring myself to eat. I have also felt that many people go to the synagogue because having been brought up to do so, they somehow feel they are expected to go. But I've always thought true religion is basically a way of life. It's more important not to harm other people in any way than to pay lip-service by attending services regularly. It's the intent that matters, not the mere observance of customs.

But the odd thing is that frequently when I go abroad, the first thing I do is to find out if there is a synagogue nearby. And there was one in Nairobi, I learnt to my surprise. So one Friday evening I put on my hat, wandered around and found a medium size, beautifully built building with a large stone tablet outside inscribed 'Nairobi Hebrew Congregation'. It was not very large but was most impressively decorated. I learnt later that it had been designed by a German-Jewish architect who had fled from Hitler's persecutions.

Two dozen men and a dozen or so women were sitting and waiting for the service to commence. It was just the same as those I recall from my youth. I couldn't get over my feeling of amazement to find a Jewish congregation in Nairobi. During the service I was motioned by the officials on to the 'Bimah' or reading desk and honoured by being invited to read the 'Kiddush' prayer (the ceremonial benediction of the wine). They probably wanted to see whether the new visitor could read Hebrew. This I did without difficulty because, as part of my orthodox upbringing, I had learnt to read it quite fluently, and have never forgotten it. Chatting to various members of the congregation after the service I was interested to learn that the actual membership of the synagogue was fairly small and that the quorum, or 'Minyan', needed for services were usually made up by visitors to Nairobi. Indeed, I was told that the congregation that morning included three Israelis, two Americans, a Canadian, a Hungarian, two Australians, a New Zealander, a German and myself. The rest were local people. Some of the visitors were members of aircrews, and others were international businessmen. Because of the smallness of the local community, they could not afford a minister or rabbi. Each service, whether on Friday night, Saturday or on high holydays was conducted by a volunteer, who also did the reading. I spoke to the youngish man who had

110

officiated very ably that morning and was amazed to learn that he was an American from Chicago, and the consultant cardiologist at Nairobi Hospital.

The president of the synagogue was an Englishman who'd been living in Nairobi for some years. He invited me to his house for dinner after service the following Friday evening. This would not interfere with my show at the hotel as that usually started about eleven o'clock. Accordingly, I went to the Friday evening service and was told there would be some other guests, among whom would be his very good friend Father Kelly, a Catholic priest. While waiting after the service to find out in whose car I would be travelling (we are not supposed to travel by car on the Sabbath day, so obviously they were not all that orthodox in Nairobi) I found myself talking to an elderly Jewish lady who'd originally come from Odessa in Russia, the town in which my father had lived as a young man. Somehow we began talking in Yiddish. To think I had come all the way to Nairobi to talk Yiddish to a woman from *der Heim*!

But that was not all. My host asked me to join up with a man who was also a guest, and I would be driven in his car to the house. He was bearded and Semitic in appearance. I was very surprised when he introduced himself as Father Kelly.

My host was obviously a very religious man. There were many things in his house which reminded me of orthodox homes. When we sat down to dinner, prayers were recited and the Sabbath candles lit before food was served. Everything kosher in the house was flown in from Israel. The guests had been chosen as much for their varied religions as for their personal charm. The host, the lady who had been a German refugee and I were Jewish. At the foot of the table was Father Kelly. The other guests were a young couple, a beautiful young Hindu lady and her Muslim husband. During the course of the conversation, which inevitably included a good deal of comment about our different religions, the young couple told us that they had both been cut off by their respective families for having married out of their own faiths. And I thought that sort of thing happened only among Jews and Catholics. Father Kelly, who was working at Nairobi University teaching 'comparative religion', had a busy time answering our questions.

One of the trips arranged for us was going on safari to *Treetops*, the celebrated nature reserve with the hotel built in the upper branches of enormous trees. Surprisingly, it had a very high degree of comfort. There was a spacious lounge complete with bar, a large dining-room, with many small bedrooms. The atmosphere was unique. Tree-trunks protruded through the floor here and there, and visitors had to climb specially built staircases like ladders. A feature of the hotel was a verandah extending all the way round the outside of the building, where guests could sit and watch the wild life emerging from the surrounding forest at any time of the day or night to use the nearby waterhole. At night, faint amber lights allowed the guests to see the animals, which were completely unaware of the many eyes watching them. I was lucky enough to see herds of elephants, wilde-beasts, zebras and wart-hogs; and of course, countless numbers of baboons, which were everywhere, even climbing the sides of the hotel and looking in through the bedroom windows. An official hunter was always on duty, armed with a loaded rifle in case of prowling lions.

Late one night, as many of us were keeping a look-out on the verandah, there was an unusual incident. We were always requested to keep our voices very low so as not to disturb the animals, and there were notices asking photographers not to use flash when taking pictures. A herd of elephants consisting of one bull and four or five cows with their babies were drinking at the hole, their trunks stretched out like columns. Suddenly they began running hither and thither. The little ones ran to their mothers, who huddled them close and formed a protective ring. The bull-elephant wheeled round, raised his trunk straight in the air, roared loudly and began charging straight into the forest.

One of the spectators on the verandah, more knowledgeable than most, told us that the elephant was charging the hyenas who were out there in a big circle. They were hoping to attack the little ones, and if you looked carefully you could see the hyenas' eyes. Sure enough, out in the distant forest there were many pairs of eyes in an enormous circle, just like glittering dots. When the bull-elephant charged, the eyes disappeared. When he returned, the whole herd formed a long line, one behind the other like a circus act and slowly disappeared in the opposite direction. It was certainly a fascinating incident, and despite the notices forbidding the use of flash photography, this was an opportunity not to be missed.

Less happy was another excursion – to Mombasa. A safari van, a small coach covered with zig-zag stripes, was placed at our disposal, and a small party of us driven on the single road from Nairobi to Mombasa, a distance of about 250 miles. The road stretched in a perfectly straight line from one town to another. We were taken through an enormous nature reserve, and saw the terrible effects of the drought which had smitten the country. Here, many elephants had died from thirst. The trees were dead, with their trunks and branches sucked dry by the animals in their desperate search for moisture. It was a depressing sight, and it showed how puny man really is when nature decides to show her power.

While at Mombasa we were invited on board a British frigate which was lying off-shore. About ten people were invited, and all the men wore formal attire: collars and ties with jackets instead of semi-tropical casuals. The ladies wore long gowns. We were driven from the hotel to the landing stage where we were met by a pinnace with sailors standing ready to assist us aboard. It was pitch dark as we went out to sea, except for the very bright stars above. After some minutes the boat turned left in a wide sweep. As we rounded the bay, we were confronted by an unforgettable sight: the frigate, flood-lit from stem to stern, riding regally on the sea with its reflection shimmering in the water and the boat itself completely surrounded by darkness.

We were piped aboard the frigate, and were shown all over the ship by the officers, who were all in 'mufti'. Then we sat down to an excellent meal in the Officers' Mess. Conversation was animated, for they were obviously delighted to have some non-service company to talk to. We then proceeded to the ward-room, where all available armchairs had been set out in rows, and in the most pleasant of atmospheres, we watched a film about Nelson.

We stayed in Kenya for almost five weeks. On returning home, I continued freelancing for a few weeks until I went with Dickie to the famous London theatre-restaurant *The Talk of the Town*. We were there for four weeks, playing in the heart of London's West End, with the holiday-makers and travellers of the world as an audience. It was a spectacular show, with a big band, lots of girls in colourful exotic costumes, and fabulous sets.

Then there was the Yarmouth summer season. That was also quite a bill. With Dickie as the star, there were supporting acts like Edmund Hockridge, Peter Goodwright and others, all names in the world of show business. The social scene was also exciting. I even went to some race meetings for the first time. The weather was glorious. Pearl and Simon also came and we all lost money together.

November 1975 saw me back again in Nairobi with Dickie. He was a very keen golfer, and for this visit had helped to organize a charity match between an English team and a team from Nairobi. The English side consisted of three well-known variety acts: Dickie himself, Teddy Peiro (an Argentine juggler and musical entertainer), Hope and Keen (a double act), plus three top ranking professional golfers and two famous sporting celebrities, Henry Cooper and Bobby Charlton. I do not play golf. I was invited along because on the last evening of the ten day tour, there would be a banquet at the New Stanley Hotel, at which the artistes would perform their acts. I would supply the musical accompaniment. I would also be required to play music very quietly while the banqueters were dining. The proceeds from the meal were going to a charity for disabled and crippled young children.

The fun began when our plane touched down at Nairobi Airport. We were beseiged by the local newsreel reporters and the general press, all of whom had been told to welcome the famous golfers from England. By chance I was the first to descend the steps from the plane. I could see all the cameras pointing at me, or so it seemed, while the reporters called out 'Welcome to Nairobi. Can you tell us what clubs in England you play for and what is your handicap?' I felt very embarrassed as I stood on the tarmac surrounded by reporters. They thought I was joking when I told them I don't play golf. During this visit another trip to Mombasa was arranged, and one of the high spots was an open-air dinner given for the whole of the golfing party. The tables were beautifully laid and a small jazz group of African musicians played old standard numbers discreetly in a corner. The main course was a superb lobster salad. It was one of those occasions when I had to make a deliberate effort to eat shellfish. I must confess that it was not unpleasant! The service was excellent, though the whole time I kept asking myself what a nice Jewish boy was doing here in Mombasa, eating lobster under the stars!

High life (con spiritoso) and coda

By this time Dickie and I, with our constant travelling, were getting rather concerned about the standard of performance at engagements, particularly at some of the clubs. We would be told beforehand that there was a seven, eight or nine piece band highly recommended and ready to play for us. Often they sounded quite good, especially when playing with a disco beat (the young musicians knew all the tunes which were top of the charts). But in actual fact, they were only playing what they already knew. When I handed the band-books to the instrumentalists, I would hear what became the dreaded words: 'I'm not a very good reader, but after I've heard the tune a couple of times I'll be able to follow. I pick up tunes very quickly.' We couldn't risk doing our shows with the musicians 'following' us and Dickie decided that as we always carried our own drummer, Terry FitzGerald, and bass-guitarist Tony Smith, we should in future always be our own self contained unit, accompanying Dickie's act as a trio. And very successful it was too. If he decided to switch routines or make a change during the show, there was no need for him to tell us; we knew exactly what was happening and played accordingly.

May brought another exciting trip abroad: to Oman in the Persian Gulf. This was organized by Combined Services Entertainment for the purpose of giving shows to RAF personnel stationed at two air bases, Masirah and Salala, last staging posts between England and India in the days of Empire. We flew out from Brize Norton in Oxfordshire, all the passengers seated facing the tail of the plane as the RAF considers it safer to travel that way. It was the first time I had visited an Air Force base since I was demobbed in 1945. Now I did not have to salute anybody, and was amused to be addressed by sergeants and corporals as 'Sir', so different from when I had to jump to it years before.

In addition to playing for Dickie, our trio was required to back the supporting acts. We were presenting a package show: that is, a complete, self-contained entertainment unit. A rehearsal was therefore necessary. The hall had no roof; neither did the stage. As we sat rehearsing, the sun blazed down on us and the heat frequently became unbearable. This was at Masirah, which is actually an island south-east of Oman. We did a couple of nights there and were then flown to Salala, where we repeated the performances. Though the camps were literally built in deserts and wilderness, the men living in such inhospitable regions had managed to devise ways of spending their leisure time.

One night, after our show, some of the officers arranged a 'Crab Derby'. They caught a number of crabs, and each one was placed under a mug at the end of a stretch of ground about ten feet long and marked off into separate lanes, one mug to a lane. They were given typical race-horse names, odds were laid on them, with one officer running the 'book'. At the call the mugs were raised and the crabs started crawling in all directions. They moved here, there, right, left, anywhere except in a straight line, much to the amusement of the spectators. Eventually a crab crossed the finishing line amid great cheers. What happened to them afterwards I do not know.

Each camp had a magnificent swimming pool always open to off-duty personnel. Masirah even had its own radio station where visitors were interviewed by the officer in charge. These interviews were really 'chat shows', and I was the guest on one occasion. I was also persuaded to play the organ, a beautiful little electronic instrument, for a church service. Just as some months previously I had asked myself what was I doing in Mombasa eating lobster, so once again as I was playing I asked myself what a nice Jewish boy was doing here in Masirah playing the organ for a church service.

The trip to Salala was notable above all for the incident of the turtles. An off-duty outing was arranged and we journeyed by van from one side of the island to the other, where there was a most beautiful beach. To reach this, we travelled through one of the most desolate tracts of country I've ever seen; no roads as such, just a fantastic landscape of rocks and boulders, with steep cliffs on either side. The men called it 'The Valley of the Moon', and as we rode precariously over this terrain, the vans tilting and jolting, we wondered whether the trip was worth the discomfort.

There were a few isolated villages of tin huts, the villagers poverty stricken with little food or water in their region. They knew that every time RAF personnel came by, they could be sure of being given sandwiches and drinks. So out they came from their houses, running towards us, cheering and waving at the men who always stopped to distribute their largesse.

The children were first to arrive, followed by women wearing long black garments and with their faces heavily veiled. They were forbidden to come out and meet strange men, but their own menfolk were away working and the need to get extra food made them ignore their customs. They would collect all that the visitors could spare and wait around patiently hoping for more. The little boys were very cheeky in a pleasant way. One came up to me, grinning and obviously trying to be friendly. I said 'Shalom Haleichem': Hebrew for 'Peace be unto you'. I was delighted when he answered in Arabic, 'Salaam Aleikem'.

We arrived at the beach, where we stayed until well after nightfall. It was a beautiful place. We placed the vans close together and hung some material between them to act as an awning for shelter from the heat of the sun. One of the servicemen had told us this was the season when the giant turtles came out of the sea to lay their eggs in the sand, and it was a sight we shouldn't miss. We waited around until it was dark, just wandering up and down the beach. We didn't really expect to see anything, but unbelievably, one of the men who had gone off by himself waved his torch at us and called out that he'd found one. Sure enough, there in the light of the torch was a huge turtle slowly waddling from the sea to a spot about thirty yards inland. Ignoring the light, it selected a suitable spot and began digging away in the sand with its rear flippers to make a large hole. We were fascinated. Then to our amazement several more giant turtles slowly made their way from the sea up the beach and repeated the motions of the first. When the holes were deep enough, they stopped digging and remained still to lay their eggs. Eventually, they clambered up and carefully scraped the sand back to cover them up. They clambered clumsily out of the holes and, completely ignoring us, very slowly waddled straight back into the sea and swam off. We watched them by the light of several torches which had somehow magically

117

appeared. Mystified, we were left to wonder how they knew where to go, what to do about preparing the right type of hole and what they did having laid their eggs.

Back in England, I continued to find 1976 a particularly busy and eventful year. The summer season was spent at Clacton; but I was also playing the organ on the band-stand for my old friend Les Cullen at Southend. For several weeks I commuted between the two resorts – a distance of about sixty miles each way. I left in the morning, did my organ show in the afternoon, and then tore back to Clacton. All went well, despite some anxious moments when the holiday traffic became particularly heavy.

Then I was off again with Dickie, to Cyprus. This was another CSE engagement and was more like a holiday than work, for Cyprus is a beautiful island, with ideal weather. As before we were required to accompany the other acts, and the show was held in the open. Tables were set out as in a theatre-restaurant, and the atmosphere resembled that of an exclusive club with a first-class cabaret.

I returned from Cyprus on a Friday. Two days later we were on a plane bound for Paris. The engagement was at the celebrated *Crazy Horse Club*, whose tableaux and productions of nude shows are world famous. Not that I was to appear in any of them: the customers might have had something to say about that. The club's owner was making a film to advertise the international aspect of their productions, and Dickie had been engaged to do one little spot, his famous impression of a drunk trying to sing like Sinatra. The idea was similar to that of the Baden-Baden engagement. However, when we arrived, we found the stage was so small that there was not even room for an upright piano. So I recorded the accompaniment on tape. Dickie had to work each show to a fixed tempo routine, which was extremely difficult. Then, after a few pleasant days in Paris, it was back to the non-glamorous freelancing in London, but not for long. A fortnight later I was off again to a place which was now beginning to be a commuter hop from home, Nairobi.

The New Stanley Hotel had discontinued its policy of having cabaret artistes in the Grill Room, and for the last month of the old regime they had a special 'super' menu and brought Dickie back as their 'Ultimate Cabaret Artiste', a clever play on words. By now, of course, we knew many people there and were welcomed back enthusiastically. I visited my friends from the previous trip and was entertained at the British Club, an institution whose colonial decor, pictures of royalty, cane armchairs and soft-footed waiters were straight out of the world of Somerset Maugham. Trips were again organised for us to visit *Treetops* and Mombasa, places just as exciting as on our previous visits. The month flew by, and the last night was memorable, though tinged with sadness at the thought that we were unlikely to visit the hotel again. All too soon it was early November, and we were back home.

Then Dickie appeared at the London Palladium for a month, an engagement coinciding with another for the same period at the Savoy Hotel. This was just about the most prestigious engagement I've ever had: to appear on the stage of the world's most famous variety theatre conducting the Palladium orchestra, and then go off to one of the great hotels to repeat the process. I felt this was a pinnacle of success in my particular part of the profession.

The next main engagement was at the Palace Theatre, Manchester, where I was MD for the panto *Babes in the Wood*. This had been in Bristol the previous winter, and it was a spectacularly lavish production with the same principals: Dickie as Nicholas, Arthur Askey as the Dame and Mark Wynter as Robin Hood, plus a very large number of Merry Men, villagers, dancers and singers, and an orchestra of about twelve or so musicians. It was a first-class production in every way, but business was not as good as anticipated. By coincidence, there were a number of other pantos around the fringes of Manchester. Whatever their standard, they all helped to divert the paying customers from us, and the children really did not know they were seeing only second-rate shows. But that's the way it is in show business: on some you win, on others you lose.

After the excitement of the preceding year, 1977 was largely a matter of routine organ concerts and one-nighters with Dickie up and down the country, until Southport and the summer season, starting in July. I was not the MD for the whole show, just in charge of Dickie's act when, as usual, I sat at the piano on stage. On the same bill was Moira Anderson. During rehearsals we were sitting together in the stalls when she turned to me and asked: 'What am I going to do Louis? I'm not happy with the band's accompaniment. I can't face the thought of doing a whole summer show like this. Will you play for me?' I remember looking rather surprised at her. I wanted to help, but was there as Dickie's accompanist. It wouldn't be right for me to agree without his permission. Later on I spoke to him about it. 'I always like to help a fellow-artiste,' he said, 'and I don't mind if you play for Moira's act, but you can't be on stage playing the piano for her and then later on, be seen as my accompanist.'

And so it was arranged that I accompanied her from the pit, directing the musicians from there and later in the show appearing on stage. It was a satisfactory arrangement all round: the producer paid me extra money for this work, the band was relieved of the responsibility of the accompaniment and Moira was very satisfied. It reminds me of how many times I've helped out in this way at concerts, when the pianist couldn't cope with anything other than a strict four beats to the bar. It's surprising how many musicians can't play a piece of music unless they are tapping their foot to keep themselves in tempo. Give them a *rallentendo* or *rubato* passage and they're lost.

The summer show finished in early September and we went straight up to Glasgow for a week at the King's Theatre and a week in Kirkcaldy in Fifeshire. The theatre was the Adam Smith Centre. Little did I know what a difference one week there would make to my professional life. The manager, Chris Potter, had recently taken over the directorship of the theatre. He loved show business, had been a drama teacher and was now very determined to put his theatre on the map. He was excellent company and full of ideas. We had quite a few chats during the week, though only of the ordinary kind indulged in by travelling artistes and musicians.

Some weeks later, I received a surprise phone call from Chris. It appeared that he was producing the forthcoming Christmas panto at the theatre and was also writing the script. He was anxious to find an organist for this production. Previous pantomimes had used only a piano and drums, and he wanted to change this by having an organ and drums. It had occurred to him that as I was an organist, I would probably know of someone suitable who might be interested. I asked him to give me some details of the engagement such as length of run, number of performances, and the proposed salary. When he had done so, I felt so interested that I offered to do it myself. I discussed the matter with Dickie. I felt that I would not be breaking faith if I went to Kirkcaldy instead of going with him to his pantomime, because as in every production of this kind, he simply becomes one of the characters in the story. I, as MD, would have to learn the new script, with its new music cues. In fact, Dickie was quite happy to let me go for the panto season, and to carry on together afterwards as before.

We still had another trip to do together beforehand, however. It was in November and we went to Northern Ireland to give shows to the British troops. Until then I had no idea what security really meant. We were met at the airport and escorted by armed soldiers to a hotel just outside Belfast. In the town itself I saw an iron railing stretched across the pavements, separating pedestrians and shutting off all traffic. People queued at the gates in the railings to cross into the other section of the street, were searched before they were allowed through into the shopping areas, and were searched again at the entrance to each shop. At the hall where we did our show, the audience, made up entirely of soldiers, sat at tables with their loaded rifles always at hand. They wore camouflage suits and were continually coming and going on their duties. Some of the troops were very young. It looked like a film set, with soldiers carrying rifles all the time; except those guns were real.

At night, after the show, we were entertained to a meal in the Officers' Mess. The enormously long table was beautifully laid with magnificent silver pieces, the excellent food served by Army waiters in the atmosphere of a very dignified and exclusive country club. I was privileged to sit between the Commanding Officer and the Intelligence Officer (Dickie was on the CO's right). Chatting to them, I could not help thinking that sort of situation never occurred to me during my RAF days.

In early December, I made my way up to Kirkcaldy to commence rehearsals for the panto *Mother Goose*. The show was amusing, though not as lavish as the previous year at Manchester. The theatre was much smaller, and I did not have an orchestra at my disposal. But our accompaniment was excellent, everybody was pleased, and Chris and I got on very well together.

In the event, this journey in 1977 was the forerunner of numerous visits I was to make. For my second panto, *Babes in the Wood*, Chris asked me to write some songs to his own lyrics. These were so well liked that for all future pantos I was asked to write all the songs. And subsequently, I've been there playing for pantos and other presentations, including some of my own, no fewer than seventeen times.

One of Chris' friends, a doctor named Kerr Hay, was particularly friendly towards the company. Realizing that quite a number of the artistes lived a long way from Kirkcaldy and would be unable to get home for Christmas to be with their families, he and his wife Joan held open house. Members of the company were invited to spend the day with them, doing more or less as they pleased. We were fed magnificently, watched TV, and ended up with singing round the piano for which, naturally, I was the pianist.

In addition to the lofty and important types of work just mentioned, I continued playing in humbler capacities. In the early part of 1978 for example, I acted as a rehearsal pianist for a forthcoming musical production of *Annie* (the musical version of the famous American cartoon 'Little Orphan Annie') which was due to open at the Victoria Palace. Organ broadcasts also continued, though thinner on the ground than before and mostly for concerts organized by cinema-organ societies.

Overall, there was definitely a change taking place in the world of freelancing and of summer seasons. One-night engagements were noticeably decreasing in number. Because of the general economic situation in the country, with unemployment on the increase, inflation rising steeply and the cost of living going up, many people just did not have the money to go to seaside resorts for their summer holidays; or if they did, they preferred to go abroad on one of the many package deals, where they could be reasonably sure of getting what they wanted most – sunshine.

Although the really big artistes and groups could still draw huge crowds at their concerts, the non-pop world was beginning to find things rather different. With rare exceptions, many named artistes could not draw the money-paying public. After all, why spend money on going to a show when they could always be seen on TV? Even the bigger clubs, and some venues which normally ran shows for a full week, now presented them for three or four day bookings only, and sometimes only for weekends.

But despite the recession and the difficult times, there were still many youngsters eager to enter this precarious profession and determined to make it to the top. Meanwhile, my own professional life continued along its by now familiar path.

1978 saw me travelling up and down the country, from Kirkcaldy down to the Channel Islands. The list of places reads like a guide book: Bath, Sheffield, Yeovil, Southampton, Gloucester, Cardiff. So it went on. The rehearsals for *Annie* were in March and April. Dickie was not doing a summer season that year so I was free to accept other

was not doing a summer season that year so I was free to accept other engagements. For the summer I went again to Southport. This show featured Windsor Davies and Don Estelle, two successful performers in the TV series *It ain't half hot mum*.

The summer of 1979 was divided between the Isle of Wight and Felixstowe, as Dickie's accompanist, while the panto *Jack and the Beanstalk* was again at Kirkcaldy. The following summer of 1980 was spent at Ilfracombe, where the star was my old friend Ted Hockridge. He had his own pianist, Jack Martin, and we quickly established a musical rapport. Our joint accompaniment, together with the drummer, was highly praised. (We were, I should say are, experienced musicians and members of the old school, not just chord-symbol players.) In the summer of 1981 I was back again in Ilfracombe, but with an even smaller scale show than the previous year. The older I became, the smaller the orchestra I was given; a trio last year, this year just organ and drums. How different from the days when I conducted an orchestra of fourteen at Bournemouth.

Despite the general gloom of the time, two outstanding trips provided highlights in the general pattern of freelancing. The first was in October 1978: a visit with Dickie to Hong Kong.

Of course the very name conjures up pictures of an exotic region. It is truly a magical place with its mixture of modern influences and concrete culture; its buildings and office blocks, a beautiful harbour and interior mountainous regions, and the old tenement buildings, crowded streets and colourful shops of the old city.

The engagement was at the celebrated Mandarin Hotel, amongst the most famous in the world. We were met at the airport and driven to the hotel, where the manager and his entourage were waiting for us in the vestibule. We were greeted like nobility. We were all introduced – Dickie, his wife Gwyneth and myself – and everybody shook hands most courteously. I was introduced to a young lady who was the Public Relations Officer. She spoke fluent English as well as Chinese, and I was somewhat surprised when she said to me, 'Oh, Mr Mordish, I have an apology to make to you.' I looked bewildered. 'I couldn't have your stationery printed as I didn't know your name, but if you give it to me in full, I'll see to it straight away.' It turned out that the hotel always presented printed stationery for special visitors. I gave her my name and sure enough, next morning there was pushed under my door a thin box containing stationery with the words printed

123

at the bottom of each sheet: 'from Louis Mordish at the Mandarin Hotel'.

I spent five weeks in Hong Kong, enjoying every moment of my stay. An English couple, a tutor at the Technical College and his wife, took me under their wings and showed me around, taking me to places I would not otherwise have known about. There were frequent trips by ferry boat across to the shopping centre at Kowloon, and a visit to 'The Temple of a Thousand Buddhas', reached by climbing hundreds of stone steps built into the mountainside. I also visited Aberdeen, where the people live on boats, and of course to the top of 'The Peak' with its magnificent panorama of the city.

I was amazed to find a well-built, oldish synagogue which could have been in England except for the vestibule. There plaques were inscribed to the memory of those who gave their lives in the War against the Japanese, names like Cohen and Goldberg. I felt so strange when I read them. It made me realize more than ever how the last war was in actual fact a World War, and not just confined to Europe.

It was Succoth, the Festival of the Tabernacles. I met an elderly man who had left Czechoslovakia thirty-three years previously and had lived in Hong Kong ever since. He was now a widower, had retired from work and lived alone. He was joined by several young men; some were Australians, others Israeli. They had all come into the Succah, the special booth constructed for the Festival, to say the appropriate blessings for the Holy Days and to drink some Festival wine. Afterwards, I had a long walk with this man through the streets and listened to his fascinating stories about the treatment of the Jews during the War, how he had left his native land to make a new home in this part of the world, and how even in Hong Kong there had been so many remarkable changes since his arrival. When we touched on the religious side of his life, I was struck as ever by the fact that although our homes were thousands of miles from each other, on opposite sides of the globe, our backgrounds and ideas were so similar.

The second outstanding trip was in February 1982, to Bahrain, an island just off the mainland of Saudi Arabia. Dickie and our little self-contained unit had been engaged as the cabaret artistes at the Gulf Hotel. This was a very modern establishment, exuding luxury and wealth. All the guests seemed to be important business people, most of them Arabs in colourful costumes. At that time a great deal of land reclamation was taking place with luxury hotels springing up everywhere. The Gulf Hotel was one of these fairly new buildings.

It seemed that because of the dreadful situation in Lebanon where civil war and invasion had created havoc, many of the big financial houses were transferring everything from the devastated areas of Beirut to Bahrain. The big new modern luxury hotels rising all around were being built to accommodate the large numbers of international business people and were competing with each other by providing cabaret entertainment for their English-speaking guests. The engagement was most enjoyable and interesting and as usual was in the late evening, leaving us the whole of the day to ourselves. I wandered through the town on a number of occasions, with its mixture of ancient markets and bazaars and modern Western buildings, as in Hong Kong. Different nations with different ideologies, traditions and customs, but all people with the same basic needs and desires. Nevertheless, I should add in passing that I did not enquire whether there was a synagogue in Bahrain!

On my return to England, I carried on very much as before: cabaret with Dickie, summer shows and Christmas pantomimes, organ broadcasts and concerts. Altogether it was a gentlemanly and civilized way of earning a living. However this pleasant way of life sustained a nasty jolt in the autumn of 1985 when Dickie was taken ill.

A few weeks later he was dead. I was shattered when I heard the news. Quite apart from the fact that I had been his Musical Director and pianist for fourteen years, we had become very good friends. He was a man whom I admired immensely, not only for his many talents as an entertainer but also as a person.

My last engagement with him had been at the famous Gleneagles Hotel in Scotland. The following morning at breakfast, he said, 'Let's go for a walk round the golf-course, it's such a lovely day.' As we strolled along leisurely, he remarked, 'Isn't it beautiful here – makes you feel good to be alive.' He appeared to be savouring the joys of such surroundings and seemed in no hurry to get back to London. In retrospect, it was as though he had a premonition of the future.

We flew down to Heathrow, took a taxi into town, parted at Paddington station – and that was the last time I saw him.

His passing obviously left a sizeable gap in my professional life. I remember thinking 'What happens now?' There is very little middle-of-the-road music to speak of these days and I certainly don't belong to the modern generation of keyboard players – for which, dare I say it, I'm grateful.

I'm old-fashioned enough to believe that a performer should perform: that is, use his hands for playing an instrument to make music and not to twiddle knobs on an electronic device for making noises. And here I would like to emphasize the difference between sounds which enhance music and sound for sound's sake. It might be argued that even the cinema organ in its day produced new sounds. True up to a point. But I would contend that those 'new' sounds were natural and used with discretion, and actually enhanced the musical standard of the composition. Modern electronic sounds are often synthetically contrived and are frequently used because they are new and different, with little musical bearing on the work. I would add, however, that the use of certain types of electronically produced sounds are most effective at times, as for instance in certain cases, when weird or supernatural effects are desired. In horror films they can be quite spine-chilling and hair-raising.

At the time, I felt that short of a miracle, there could be very little in the way of further work to excite me, not that I'm blasé, but facts are facts. I've played so many different kinds of music for so many different kinds of entertainment and entertainers, that anything I might do in the future could only be a repetition in some form or another of something I've already done in the past.

But miracles do happen – even though they are comparatively minor! One day, out of the blue, I received a phone call from someone I'd never met asking whether I'd be interested in an engagement as pianist at the famous Claridge's Hotel in Mayfair. I was happy to accept, and now play the same kind of music I played many years ago at the Kit-Kat restaurant and with the BBC Grand Hotel Palm Court Orchestra. My musical wheel has almost turned full circle!

I am no longer in the first flush of youth and although I do not play on the organ as much as I used to, I am nevertheless full of confidence in its future as a means of entertainment because of the encouraging number of young organists who are taking to the instrument. Their world of theatre organ playing can obviously never be the same as in my younger days in the 'golden age' of super-cinemas, but happily the instrument can and does function equally well in 'concert' surroundings.

I remain as active in my profession as circumstances will allow, playing at Claridge's, freelancing in various hotel lounges, occasionally accompanying artistes, and giving the ever enjoyable organ concerts – wherever they take place. Long may they all continue!